RESOURCES FOR EDUCATIONAL RESEARCH AND DEVELOPMENT

A Report of the
National Foundation for Educational Research
in England and Wales

Resources for educational research and development

A. Vernon Ward

NFER Publishing Company Ltd.

Published by the NFER Publishing Company Ltd.

Registered Office: The Mere, Upton Park, Slough, Bucks, SL1 2DQ
Book Division: 2 Jennings Buildings, Thames Avenue,
Windsor, Berks, SL4 1QS

First Published 1973

SBN 85633 026 4

Printed in Great Britain by
KING, THORNE & STACE LTD., SCHOOL ROAD, HOVE, SUSSEX BN3 5JE

Distributed in the USA by Humanities Press Inc.,
450 Park Avenue South, New York, NY 10016, USA

CONTENTS

LIST OF TABLES

LIST OF ABBREVIATIONS

ATCDE	Association of Teachers in Colleges and Departments of Education
BPS	British Psychological Society
CERN	Conseil Européen pour la Recherche Nucléaire
CILT	Committee for Instruction in Language Teaching
CRDML	Committee for Research and Development in Modern Languages
CVC	Committee of Vice Chancellors
DGRST	Délégation Generale à la Recherche Scientifique et Technique
DSIR	Department of Scientific and Industrial Research
ERIC	Educational Resources Information Center
ESEA	Elementary and Secondary Education Act
FE	Further Education
GNP	Gross National Product
HE	Higher Education
HERU	Higher Education Research Unit
HMI	Her Majesty's Inspector
IEA	International Association for the Evaluation of Educational Achievement
ILEA	Inner London Education Authority
INSEE	Institut National de Statistique et des Etudes Economiques
IPN	Institut Pédagogique National
LEA	Local Education Authority
LSE	London School of Economics
MRC	Medical Research Council
NCB	National Children's Bureau
NCET	National Council for Educational Technology
NFER	National Foundation for Educational Research
OECD	Organization for Economic Co-operation and Development
R & D	Research and Development
REL	Regional Educational Laboratories
RNIB	Royal National Institute for the Blind
RNID	Royal National Institute for the Deaf
SCRE	Scottish Council for Research in Education
SRHE	Society for Research in Higher Education
SRC	Science Research Council
SSRC	Social Science Research Council
UCET	Universities Council for the Education of Teachers
UGC	University Grants Committee
USOE	United States Office of Education
VG	Vocational Guidance

ACKNOWLEDGEMENTS

I would have wished to thank the late Dr Stephen Wiseman for introducing me to the area of educational R & D, and encouraging me to explore the literature. I wish to thank Professor Mark Blaug for suggesting certain lines of attack in the more difficult sections of the work, and for helping me on related although different problems.

I must thank the Directorate of the NFER for advice and encouragement during this rather protracted study, and for dealing with the interests of an economist in such an understanding manner.

Finally, I must thank my secretary, Mrs Diana Davis, who dealt with much of the early work of the project and, not least, managed to transform an often illegible manuscript into a recognizable draft.

Introduction

Interest in the volume and nature of resources available for educational research and development (R & D) has no doubt existed for as long as educational research has been pursued. In recent years, however, there has been an intense concern for the funds and manpower invested in R & D and much discussion of the costs and benefits of R & D in the social sciences generally and in education in particular (for discussion of definitions of research and development, see Chapter 2). That interest should extend so far as to include not only academic, but political and public interest, is a reflection both of the importance of education, and of the climate of opinion in which funds for R & D are made available.

A rationale for Government funding of R & D has long depended on the assertion that the economic benefits of research are positive, although this assertion often relies upon identifying 'spin-offs' which are derivatives of the basic area of inquiry (Rose and Rose, 1970). The science lobby has had a longer and more urgent need to provide a refined rationale but the social sciences and education are likely to require some detailed reflections on the subject very soon (Jenkins and Velody, 1970; SSRC, 1968/70; Taylor, 1971). This project deals briefly with some aspects of the subject, but its prime aim is to provide the data on resources, projects, and sponsors which are essential pre-requisites of any subsequent inquiry into the criteria for R & D allocation.

The earliest estimates of resources available for R & D in education were made by Dr Wall in his address to the National Association of Inspectors and Education Organizers (NAIEO) in 1959. He compared the sums made available to the Medical Research Council (£3·5m), the Agricultural Research Council (£4·5m) and the grants distributed through the Department of Scientific and Industrial Research (DSIR)—£12·25m—with his estimate of £0·1m available to educational research. This sum was made up of the NFER budget, the Scottish Council for Research in Education budget, and his estimates of University work in both research and post-graduate teaching in education. Expressed as a percentage of the total expenditure on education in 1958, this represented about 0·01 per cent.

By 1967, he considered that the volume of educational research expenditure had risen to about 30 times the 1958 figure—about £3m—which, when compared with the then current rate of educational expenditure, represents 0·12 per cent (Wall, 1968). This figure looks a little optimistic, but certainly there has been an expansion of interest in and funds for educational research in the last decade. Several factors have contributed to this expansion.

The first, and perhaps the most significant, factor has been the series of reports prepared by the Committees of Inquiry which have investigated the main areas of the educational system from the Crowther Report (CACE, 1959), to the Plowden Report (CACE, 1967). One of the main characteristics of all of these reports was the recognition that research work was essential in order to provide a firm base for their conclusions and recommendations. This is nowhere more strikingly shown than the Robbins Report which has left as an almost permanent legacy the Higher Education Research Unit at the London School of Economics.

The serious gaps in our knowledge revealed by the reports have had an effect mainly at the national level in that work has been generated by the Department of Education and Science (DES), the Social Sciences Research Council (SSRC), and the Universities rather than at the Local Educational Authority (LEA) level. This partly reflects the more basic nature of some of the research, partly the national character of the work, e.g. on comprehensive education, manpower planning, curriculum studies, etc., and partly the lack of resources available for research in LEAs and schools. The reports focused attention not only on our lack of knowledge, but also on the influence that education has on economic growth, on social change, and personal development, and the relatively low share of resources devoted to the education sector. Since 1960, resources have been devoted to education on an ever-increasing scale, particularly to higher education, where the demand seems greatest, the economic benefits seem more directly measurable, and where the political and policy pressures seem greatest.

The second factor affecting educational research is the simple but effective pressure of scarce resources. Total expenditure on education has increased from £810m (1958/59) to £2,157m (1968/69) and takes 6·2 per cent of the Gross National Product (GNP) in 1968/69 education statistics (DES, 1969). Clearly, if resources are to be made available, the authorities require evidence that the policy is sound and the implementation effective. It is perhaps for this reason that much R & D expenditure has been allocated to examine higher education, where the resources are high in relation to student numbers and where benefits seem to be more easily assessed. Qualified manpower is seen as an important element in economic growth and much attention has been paid to the problems of securing a balance between the demand and supply of suitably trained specialists. The problem is particularly true of scientific and engineering manpower, but may also be applied to forecasts of teacher supply. There are other areas which absorb large shares of educational resources and as expenditure grows, so will inquiries be undertaken to assess the purpose, costs, and effectiveness of this expenditure.

The third factor influencing educational R & D is the nature of educational decision making. Until recently, decision making has been carried out with a maximum of good intentions and a minimum of information concerning the economic and social consequences of educational change. This is true of all levels from DES through LEAs and the universities to individual schools. Many decisions about such matters as teacher training, the organization of schools, the care of handicapped children, and the length of compulsory schooling have been taken in the last decade without the publication of any careful appraisal of the likely benefits and costs of the proposals, or of some evaluation of the consequences of the decisions. Clearly, the decisions have been taken in good faith and with much experience and consideration, but faith is no substitute for evidence and it seems now to be recognized that major decisions require detailed investigation, both before and after such decisions are made and implemented. As Wall remarks, '. . . nor can we evade the clear responsibility of checking, in some objective way, on what we do and of attempting to make an objective study of the consequences of our decisions' (Wall, 1959). It is possible for some decisions to draw on a substantial body of information which would allow a careful appraisal of the probable consequences to be undertaken. Other decisions can be piloted: experimental changes in organization or curriculum can be made and the results made available before decisions on large-scale changes are made. There are, however, some decisions that must precede rather than follow research information. Evaluation of the consequences is therefore crucial so that modification can be made to improve and ease change as it takes place. It is unlikely that the decisions would be reversed but at least evaluation of the educational changes would be available to guide subsequent developments. Something is perhaps needed like the intended US pattern of evaluated educational change where a research programme designed to monitor and evaluate policy changes is sometimes instituted as change takes place (see Stufflebeam *et al.*, 1971).

The dual problems of a forced rate of educational change and the substantial scale of the resources involved have caused the decision-makers to consider and evaluate decisions more carefully, and as far as possible to anticipate them by planning and forecasting both change and the related expenditure. This was seen as essential at national level and in 1962 a Research and Intelligence Unit was established which was absorbed into the newly-created Planning Branch within DES. A major purpose of this branch was to initiate and encourage research work, and the gradual expansion of educational research can be traced from the sums spent—about £20,000 in 1962 to about £70,000 in 1963/4 to about £350,000 in 1969/70 (see discussion in Boyle and Crosland, 1971, p. 71).

The universities, too, responded to the tasks of expansion imposed on them by the impact of Robbins (DES, 1963). Ashby has indicated the normal methods of university decision-making—'All over the country these groups of scholars who would not make a decision about the shape of a leaf or the derivation of a word . . . make decisions about admission policy, size, staff-student ratios . . . based on dubious assumptions, scrappy data and mere hunch' (Ashby, 1963, quoted in Blaug, 1969). There has since been a considerable expansion in the information gathering and planning activities of the University Grants Committee (UGC) and the Committee of Vice-Chancellors and it is evident that in the future full use of the recent research work on higher education problems will be utilized.

It is the LEAs and schools which have yet to respond and it is probably here that some resistance is likely to be encountered. The reasons are obvious enough—resources, representing time, trained manpower, and money. It is also true that LEAs subscribe directly to research through the NFER and Schools Council. The need, however, is probably more crucial in LEAs than anywhere else. It is here that experiment and change actually take place, either through innovating heads and schools, through the work of the advisory and inspectorate staff, or through policy changes introduced through the authority. The great variety which exists in the English educational system and the autonomy available to individual heads makes change possible and yet makes evaluation difficult, although the more essential. Full advantage of these characteristics could be taken and a series of studies designed to evaluate changes and experiments which have taken place could be conducted, so that the results are available to all and the high cost of duplication and replication is avoided.

It is known that the Inner London Education Authority and Stoke-on-Trent Education Department possess Research and Intelligence Units and a few authorities probably have established or are considering the establishment of such Units. The value of such units is considerable. Apart from the regular processing of much social and educational book-keeping data (e.g. numbers and compositions of children in the authority) they can institute irregular studies of policy-making value, carry out longitudinal studies of experimental innovation and evaluate educational change within the authority (see Stoke-on-Trent Education Department, 1963). It seems the next logical step in making decisions within the largest and most expensive of local government services more effective. In the long term it is also likely to be one of the strongest forces operating upon the expansion of R & D in education.

It would be misleading to suggest that this brief sketch of growth and change in educational R & D during the last decade represents a spectacular breakthrough and that most major problems are now under investigation. An updating of Wall's figures shows that inflation has reduced much of the apparent expansion and that in percentage terms resources remain much as they were in 1959. The updated figure represents about £2·5–3m, but as educational expenditure has increased to £2,000m the percentage figure remains low at about 0·12 per cent–0·16 per cent. By comparison, the figures for Agricultural Research have increased substantially (£13·5m, 1969/70) as have those for the Medical Research Council (£15·4m). Nationally, we spend about £1,000m on R & D (1970) (DES, 1971) but making inter-industry or inter-service comparisons is not a very valuable exercise. It is true that R & D expenditure is higher in most other industries and services than in education; and it may also be true that it is unsatisfactory to find that more is spent on domestic appliances R & D in 1966/7 than on education today (1971/2) (Statistics of Science and Technology, 1970, DES and Min. Tech., 1971), but what criteria for the allocation of R & D resources can one find?

Allocation criteria for R & D resources

There is no definite answer to the general problem of how much 'should be' allocated to R & D. The question bedevils any discussion of public expenditure, and R & D expenditure is but one aspect of the general theory of allocation of funds in the public sector. For a fuller discussion of allocation criteria used by sponsors, see Chapter 3.

The first point to make clear is the current impossibility either in theory or practice of offering guidelines to the efficient allocation of public funds. There are no simple formulae for prescribing policy: to increase expenditure on education at the expense of research or defence must be based on planners' preferences which are not susceptible to economic analysis (see the general discussion in

Margolis and Guitton (1970), especially papers by Samuelson, Musgrave and Dorfman, and Blaug, 1970).

The general assumption adopted here is that a policy decision prescribes the R & D budget within which research administrators seek to optimize the allocation of funds. Given this second order allocation problem there are several models to aid the decision-maker.

The first model is the industrial R & D model: that R & D expenditures are made in the nature of an investment for which future returns are expected. Economists have been very interested in this field for some years and although the results are rather erratic and the volume of work can hardly yield definitive results, it is probably true to say that the returns to industrial R & D are positive; and that the minimum expected rate of return is of the order of 30 per cent. This allows for several failures which could easily depress the profit margins and the hope, of course, is that successful inventions will result in very high returns of up to 1,000+ per cent (Griliches, 1958, 1964; Mansfield, 1969). Apart from the obvious difficulty of placing cash values on the benefits, the objection to this model as a paradigm for allocation procedure in the social sciences and education is that to ensure a high positive rate of return the degree of uncertainty which is acceptable in industrial-based research is very low. Projects have to minimize uncertainty; and the lower the uncertainty rating, then, other things being equal, the riskless projects are selected. As a means of increasing profits and productivity this procedure is acceptable (although not necessarily optimal); as a means of advancing knowledge, improving decision-making or even of improving practice it is not at all obvious that this is the best approach.

The reasons lie in the nature of the R & D process. 'The central economic fact about the process of invention and research is that they are devoted to the production of information. By the very definition of information, invention must be a risky process in that the output (information obtained) can never be predicted perfectly from the inputs' (Arrow, 1962; also Klein & Meckling, 1958). Thus, with the level of risk and uncertainty pitched at a high level there is under-investment of resources in R & D and hence under-production of information. Given that it is impossible to calculate accurately the returns to R & D expenditure in relation to the uncertainty involved, there is a tendency for decision-makers to play safe: if the industrial model is adopted the returns would be high but much interesting and valuable research could be curtailed, or abandoned (see Jewkes *et al.*, 1969; Mansfield, 1969).

The second model is that used by the natural sciences. They have spent large sums of money on basic and applied R & D in the past two decades and some rationale for such expenditure has been discussed and elaborated, during the 'science debate' of the past 20 years. Indeed, the debate has continued until in the past ten years or so there has been something akin to a 'science policy'.

The attempt to provide a rationale which would allow some attempt at the establishment of priorities, allow the planning of research programmes and expose the criteria for choice is most easily found in the 'Minerva debate' (see Toulmin and Polanyi in *Minerva*, vol. I, 1963; vol. III, 1964; vol. II, 1964; vol. V, 1966). The basic position was outlined by Alvin Weinberg, Director of Oakridge National Laboratory in the USA (1963 and 1964). There are two criteria for choice: internal and external. The internal criteria are familiar enough—the technical excellence of the research and the immediate benefits to research fields adjacent to the subject area. In short, they represent the criteria adopted by most grant awarding bodies: is the research work good of its kind?: and is the field suitable for further work?

It is the external criterion that causes most discussion. Discussion focuses on two points: (1) are other criteria necessary at all, and (2) if so, are Weinberg's criteria the best available? The views of Polanyi (1962) aside, it seems to be considered that some criteria other than internal merit are needed: scientific research is not self-evidently justifiable on such a scale and further resources for support are needed. Weinberg's criteria are technological merit, social merit, and scientific merit.

Technological merit amounts to the argument for basic research on the areas of contemporary technological interest. Thus, if organ transplants are needed, then basic research is needed on tissue rejection. It is true that basic research may have multiple effects not least in areas other than the planned direction of research and again the chance and luck elements in discovery are important. Nevertheless, the deliberate search after a definite goal seems more likely to yield results than a vague inquiry in the unknown. The technological spin-off on basic research is important but in many ways is overrated: if one needs to justify research expenditures on these grounds there is the need to demonstrate that the spin-off would not otherwise have been invented; could not otherwise have been produced for less cost; and that the spin-offs were actually wanted or demanded by consumers.

For most of the examples usually quoted—micro circuits, solid state technology; new materials, new processes; and managerial practices—it would seem that a direct investment in such fields would have produced the same results at least as fast and probably for less cost. The argument from spin-off is weak except in Weinberg's original sense of identifying known technological requirements and diverting basic research efforts to developments which permit technological advance in that area. In educational research examples might be the need for better educational technology—of most kinds—which really require a theoretical account of learning skills before major advances can be made; or again basic research on reading skills would help in the technology and techniques of teaching reading; or again basic research on the correlates of early learning might improve the organization pattern of primary schools. In each case there is the assumption that, because technological and social benefits accrue eventually basic research in a certain area is justified.

Social and economic benefits raise other issues: most clearly matters of priority. If one had to choose between projects which were equal on other grounds, how can one judge the social value of organ transplants and hence research on immunology and the public health problem of infantile mortality in the Rhondda and Dorking (Rose and Rose, 1970)?

Granted that such choices are impossible at the margin, the fact that broad choices between subject areas must be made if funds are limited has certain implications. As the Roses argue, '... the terms in which we view what research should be supported may be seen to be generalized out into a broad critique of the values of the society in which one lives and the nature of our objectives concerning society'. What is true of science is even more true of the social sciences and education if only because funds are more limited and the choice more crucial: is education to be supported at the expense of economics or anthropology? Is, say, pre-school education to be preferred to the post-graduate sector of education? No one suggests that choice is easy, but the criteria, and implications of the criteria, need to be made clear.

Weinberg's third criterion is simple scientific merit: that basic inquiry is an integral part of man's cultural and intellectual being and must be recognized as such. Few would deny the view—expounded very clearly by Maddox (1964); Toulmin (1964); and Polanyi (1962); but the general proposition is not a decision rule for allocating £x to Science A and £y to science B, or even to allocating £n to science as a general study area. It is, however, the main argument for the £150m Conseil Européen pour la Recherche Nucléaire (CERN) nuclear accelerator. Such an argument has been refined a little to suggest that a surcharge on the technological and social based research should be made for curiosity oriented research. The size of this surcharge is nowhere definitely argued but 10 per cent on the total R & D expenditure is a favourite figure and one which is now enshrined in the official literature (Rothschild, 1971; Dainton, 1968).

If the scientists find it difficult both in theory and practice to provide decision models for allocating resources it is doubtful if educational research can show the research community how to apportion funds. Two points, however, seem to be relevant to the current difficulties of educational research. Firstly, the knowledge base from which so much development work is proceeding is very weak. It is a commonplace that the social sciences are young and immature in relation to the natural sciences: it seems to follow that a higher proportion of research funds should be devoted to basic research, curiosity oriented work, and perhaps, in education, some action oriented work. There is still the unresolved problem of what proportion this 'higher' proportion should be: and that is likely to remain unresolved.

There has been some reawakening of the science debate with the publication of the Rothschild Report on the Framework of Government R & D (HMSO, 1971) and there is now a considerable literature on the relations between the social sciences and policy making, and the relations between R & D, innovation, adoption, diffusion, and the utilization of R & D results conducted through appropriate information channels (see the reactions of the Science Research Council (SRC), and SSRC to Rothschild in *New Society*, 17.2.72; 13.1.72; Jenkins and Velody, 1970; Havelock, 1971; Stufflebeam *et al.*, 1971). The Rothschild debate is interesting but does not affect much of this report (which was substantially complete during the late summer of 1971). The customer-contractor relationship which has caused such controversy is rather reminiscent of the Secretary of State's reference (Thatcher, 1970) to a change in 'patronage' based research policy to a basis of 'commissioned' R & D in her speech to the NFER in December 1970. The design and organization of research work which is contracted for and for which Government Departments are the customer is not discussed in detail in Rothschild and yet this use of 'in-house' research is crucial to the distribution of research funds. In a closely related context the SSRC note says tartly that 'It would be a mistake, both to assume that the departments of central government are solely or even mainly responsible for interpreting the applied research needs of society, and to assert a monopolistic role for central government which would allow no place for other types of institutes in a pluralist society' (SSRC statement in *New Society*, 17.2.72). There are other points to make about the organization of R & D in the social sciences and these are discussed in Chapters 5 and 7. Although an extended discussion cannot be provided, one must mention the important work of Lindblom (Hirschman and Lindblom, 1962; Braybrooke and Lindblom, 1963; Lindblom, 1968) in which an attempt is made to build a 'realistic' theory of resource allocation and decision-making in such delicate areas as R & D, defence and economic and social policy. While it may be possible to identify the benefits of R & D, it is not usually possible to measure them in such a way that a direct relationship to costs can be expressed as a rate of return (see Blaug, 1970, particularly pp. 120–128). Cost effectiveness is thus a more appropriate instrument but it is not at all clear how the information derived from such studies is fed back to administrators and others concerned with decision makers. Lindblom's theory of disjointed incrementalism is both sceptical and convincing in its view of comprehensive, rational decision making by government and goes far to explain the present system of allocating public expenditure and formulating policies (see the discussion in Stufflebeam *et al.*, 1971).

The upshot of this brief introduction must be that there is no coherent, systematic rationale for the allocation of funds to R & D in general, nor to educational R & D in particular. The knowledge base on which such decisions are made is weak and hence it remains '*ad hoc* and partial'. 'By this I mean that it is frequently a matter of responding to events rather than anticipating and preparing for them, is usually lacking in a basis of empirical knowledge, and is always pursued without due regard to many crucial inter-relationships' (Peston in Baron & Taylor (Ed.), 1969, pp. 69–70). Until we have more information, not only as to the current pattern of R & D expenditures, but the relationship of R & D to innovation, utilization and decision-making within the educational system, there is unlikely to be much improvement.

The first step in considering the contribution of R & D to education is to provide some account of its volume and distribution and this is the prime aim of this report.

CHAPTER 1

The Resources Available

The resources for educational research and development (R & D) fall into two main categories. There is first the internal resources of manpower and finance available to the institutions carrying out R & D, and secondly, the finance made available by external sponsors. This study is almost entirely concerned with the latter category, partly because it is the largest component in the total, but also owing to the difficulties in obtaining data relating to internal funds. It is as well to make clear the terms used. 'Sponsor' refers to any body which grants funds to institutions to carry out R & D. The term covers obvious sponsors such as DES, Schools Council, etc., and the private Trusts and Foundations such as the Leverhulme Trust and the Nuffield Foundation. It also includes NFER and National Children's Bureau (NCB) because these bodies are granted funds by Local and Central Government for purposes of sponsoring R & D. In this sense the NFER is both a sponsor and performer. This can be confusing but it is hoped that the context makes clear this use of terms when discussing such bodies. 'Performers' refer to the institutions carrying out the work—the universities and the independent research institutions such as NFER, Tavistock, etc.

Having made this distinction, this chapter is concerned with the problems involved in computing the resources for R & D. The main evidence is the annual reports of the sponsoring bodies where available, and discussions with officials of Trusts and Foundations, which resulted in the release of data relating to educational projects supported by those Trusts. The sources give information relating to the title of the project supported and the size and duration of the finance made available. There are several problems attached to studies of this kind.

One difficulty is the different financial years taken by the bodies. Most institutions operate a financial year running from April 1st to March 31st, but there are others which organize their accounts by the calendar year and a few which use other dates. Clearly, some standardization was essential and it was decided to translate all accounts to a normal financial year, April 1st–March 31st. This has meant some small inaccuracies in some research projects because, instead of running from January '67–December '68, a project will be shown as operating from April '67–March '68 and from April '68–December '68, thus 'losing' three months of the project. The annual totals may therefore be somewhat misleading, but they represent the expenditures on the project in the two financial years considered. Another minor problem is that the starting date of projects was rarely given. As most projects were undertaken in universities, or similar institutions, it was decided that the allocation of funds to the project would be made in October of the year in which the funding of the project was approved. Allocation of funds is now made simple: a project funded for £10,000 over two years 1968/70 would be shown as receiving in 1968/9 £2,500 (October '68–March '69); in 1969/70 it receives £5,000; and a final £2,500 is paid in 1970/71 (April '70–September '70). Where a starting date was known (as with SSRC) then the appropriate allocation was made–dividing the duration of the project into months and apportioning it as appropriate over the project period.

This procedure has important implications. It is a deliberate attempt to achieve some measure of the annual *flows* of resources for R & D. In most cases sponsors show their research funds as part of their committed or appropriated finances and it is not uncommon to find that, say, £20,000 over two years has been allocated to a project. Clearly, £20,000 is not spent in a year and it is the *expenditure* figures which represent the flow of finance for educational research. Equally obviously, expenditure figures are difficult if not impossible to obtain and one therefore requires some formula or other procedure which will translate an appropriation account into a probable expenditure account. The procedure described above seems a suitable device. Thus, the £20,000 two-year grant becomes two annual £10,000 flows. In fact, of course, the project will probably not start until the October of the year in which the funds are granted and therefore as explained earlier, only six months' flow or £5,000 occurs in the first year; there is then a full £10,000 annual flow, and there is a final £5,000 completion for the project which occurs in a third financial year. In short, a two-year project must be allocated over three financial years because this represents the annual flow. In a few cases, notably NFER and NCB, it was more appropriate to take expenditure rather than appropriated or committed funds because these two bodies finance research work themselves and also undertake/contract research work and detailed figures were necessary to avoid confusion. It also seemed administratively easier to obtain details of expenditure rather than re-calculate committed grant figures. This distinction between committed or appropriated funds and actual expenditure can be a little confusing when one looks at the accounts of Trusts and Foundations. Some sponsors place the whole of the grant into an appropriations account at the time when the project is approved. There is thus a large divergence between committed funds and expenditure until the project gets under way and funds really begin to flow. Similarly, projects may be approved and the money laid aside in the appropriations account and yet because of under- or over-costing, or because of illness, postponements, or any of a number of other factors which affect the progress of a research project, there may be further discrepancies between committed funds and grant income. In short, in many accounts there is a divergence between research expenditures and committed or appropriations accounts. A further source of confusion can be the difference between annual grant revenue and the sums available for new work. This is clearly related to the previous point. If very large projects are funded then quite clearly the sponsor is committing future income to the project and this must have an obvious effect upon the ability to support new projects. It is a familiar enough problem to most sponsors, but one which can cause some difficulty to an outsider. One must always remember that the capacity of a sponsor to finance new projects is determined by past decision-making.

There is one final problem. Some institutions carry out work and make available the necessary resources for work which may be regarded as educational development. The resources are not large but they are nonetheless welcome. They have not been included in the analysis because the work they carry out is not strictly a project with a definite life. The Royal National Institution for the Deaf (RNID) and the Royal National Institution for the Blind (RNIB) are good examples of this problem.

Neither body has the function, nor the funds actively to sponsor educational R & D. They are, however, intimately concerned with educational problems and they both support residential centres which teach children and young adults how to learn, work, and adjust to their particular difficulties. The resources made available for this work amount to about £40,000 p.a. for RNID and about £60,000 in the case of RNIB.

The RNIB concentrates most of its development work on Larchmoor School where children are aided and guided to the point where some are able to return to normal schools, or to partially hearing schools. There is, in addition, Court Grange which helps difficult adolescent deaf boys and teaches them both a trade and 'the advantages which come with social conformity'. Most of this expenditure is probably not educational R & D, but a further £40,000 is spent at the Court Grange Training Centre and some at least must represent experimental work in the training of the boys.

The RNIB has co-operated with Birmingham University in the establishment of a research centre for the visually handicapped, and buildings and equipment worth £60,000 have been made available from the Sir Theodore Tylor Memorial Fund. This is obviously a lump sum and it is unreal to apportion it over a number of years for research projects. It is best to note it as part of the total resources available for educational research.

A final note should be made of the National Foundation for Visual Aids, which although primarily an advisory body, also contributes £7,000 p.a. to an experimental development unit. In addition, there are several bodies who cannot support R & D because of lack of funds, but who encourage and contribute to the development of work in which they see relevance and interest.

The figures indicated in Table 1.1 are probably the best available and they were collated in a rational and systematic manner, but one cannot deny that there are almost certainly some errors. There are at least three possible sources of error which anyone working with the statistics of R & D has to consider:

(1) definitions of educational research may vary;
(2) some sources of finance may have been omitted;
(3) the allocation of finance for funded projects may be inaccurate.

The first problem is one which faces any writer in the field. Two decisions are necessary—is the project research or development at all, and if so, is it Education or some other discipline? The latter problem is discussed first. The argument concerning Education as a discipline is a lengthy one and not entirely relevant to that decision (Tibble, 1966). It is clear that there *is* a subject called Education and that it can be defined narrowly or very broadly. At its narrowest it would encompass only those topics concerned with the practice of education such as curriculum studies and the organization of the education system. All other areas revert back to their parent disciplines so that learning theory becomes psychology and school–home relationships become sociology. This leaves Education as a residual subject after other disciplines have been drawn off. At the other extreme education embraces all topics which deal directly with any aspect of educational abilities and achievement, or any social, economic or physical influence on the educational system. This dramatically increases the range of topics considered 'educational'—from the medical and psychological work on abilities and disabilities of children and adults, to the economic, financial and architectural implications of educational provision.

The latter view has been chosen and the results therefore reflect the maximum number of projects and the maximum value of external finance available to the education sector. Any border-line case—and there were several—was reviewed and if any doubt existed, it was included. Most doubtful cases occurred in the medical area, particularly on work relating to handicapped children, but there is little doubt of the educational significance of such work even if some of the projects seem somewhat remote from the classroom. Similarly, the financial and economic projects have an impact on educational planning for technological and other educated manpower and have been included. Some psychological projects are clearly not 'educational' research, others equally obviously are of relevance—and the border-line cases were surprisingly few and have been included. There is also a need to distinguish subject studies from the teaching of those subjects and linguistics is a good example of that problem.

The more serious difficulty was deciding whether a project was R & D or not. Here one raises a series of problems but the major discussion of types of R & D is left until Chapter 2 and the following is simply an account of the criteria for inclusion.

A working definition of educational research may be taken as including 'those activities which are initiated within the findings and methodology of the social, behavioural and informational sciences, or are based squarely on them and which either are orientated or can be orientated toward the improvement of education and instruction' (OECD, 1969). The difficulties attached to this sort of definition or any other similar definition fall into four categories. First, the project may not strictly be R & D—it may be a bibliography or review of existing work, or a survey of practices operating in a subject or region. This has caused problems because sponsors have funded such projects. The number, duration and cost of these projects is small and hence they have been included on the grounds that they contribute to (or perhaps precede) a research or development project: that sponsors consider them to be R & D projects; and that inclusion does not cause much error in the total value of resources.

The second problem area relates to the science based nature of R & D. The traditional concept of 'science' would certainly exclude history and philosophy subjects and although more recent views (Popper, 1957; Toulmin, 1958; Walsh, 1953) would open up the debate, the matter would still give problems to a science based view of educational R & D. One is able to avoid the problem by demonstrating that very few projects in these areas are funded by sponsors and hence one can avoid the embarrassment of excluding them and/or the 'error' which may be caused by including such projects. The next chapter describes the findings of projects by subject and it may simply be stated here that there are no philosophical projects included and less than six history projects all of which involve very small sums of money.

The final problem concerns the funds available for student grants. It can be argued that post-graduate training yields R & D results and that therefore grant funds should be included in any total of resources available for educational R & D. The problem is precisely the same as that dealt with in the next section which discusses the allocation of staff time at Universities. Not all post-graduate resources represent research, particularly now that advanced reading and course work is included in post-graduate work. Student grants are therefore not included in the resources available but the sums involved (obtainable from SSRC annual reports) could easily be included if required.

The second source of error relates to the sources of finance. This problem is simply stated—there may be omissions in the list of sponsors contacted. This list is included as Appendix (2) and if further bodies do sponsor educational R & D we should be very pleased to make contact so that the results can be revised and updated. This list represents those institutions which do sponsor R & D rather than the much larger number of bodies who are interested in the work and would encourage it more actively if funds were available.

The third source of error is the allocation of funds over the project life. This problem has been discussed and errors, if any, have been consistent and systematic. In relation to the total values it is most unlikely that reallocation of project funds would make any significant difference. The two major sources of error—the different financial year and the difference between appropriation and actual project expenditure outweigh all other problems. The first has been arbitrarily adjusted to the conventional financial year and the latter has been settled in the method discussed earlier.

The method of allocation does however raise one further point. It very clearly indicates the expected flow of R & D funds each year; it is not therefore an account of committed funds. Most sponsors show their accounts as allocations, e.g. £250,000 for each year. If many projects lasted for, say, two or three years, the annual *expenditure* flow would be much less than these sums. This explains some of the variations between the figures shown later (Chapter 4) and those in the reports of some sponsors. The *committed* funds are likely to be higher (as shown in the sponsors' accounts) than those shown here because the expected *annual flow* of funds had not reached full strength in 1968/9 and 1969/70 as in the case of SSRC.

The universities and colleges

The important missing element in this assessment of research resources is, of course, the contribution made by the Universities, Colleges and Polytechnics. The difficulties attached to estimating the proportion of staff time spent on research activity are well known. The crudest of divisions lie between teaching and research, but this is unreal as staff have administrative duties, examinations, social and welfare activities, and official visits to students and others. The notion of 'research' is itself a portmanteau word which includes such items as keeping up with the subject, lecture preparation, articles and other material for publication, as well as a more restricted range of activities which are perhaps more readily identified as research. Charles Carter has summarized and clarified these items under six activities which complement teaching and offers two other areas of activity that demand staff time—artistic creation as in Music and the Arts, and the encouragement of development work on basic research discoveries (Brosan *et al.*, 1970, pp. 77–8).

Clearly, the identification of staff time allocated to research is a difficult task, but it is an important one. It has been attempted by the Committee of Vice-Chancellors and Principals (CVC), aided by the HERU at LSE, who are also undertaking a parallel study of the allocation of staff time in Polytechnics. The results of an earlier study by the UGC were rather unhappy owing to the small number of areas into which time could be classified. The new study should meet most of the objections and offers the best analysis available of the deployment and utilization of staff.

Calculating the sum involved from the University contribution to educational R & D is still quite complicated. In principle it is simple if arbitrary: one takes the mean or median or mid-incremental point, of the salaries paid to staff in university departments; multiplies by the number of staff involved; and then calculates the value of staff time devoted to research. In practice it is a rather more complex procedure. The CVC data (1972) were drawn from a sample of about 800 university staff of whom 3·6 per cent were in Education Departments. The data show that staff in Education Departments spent 18 per cent of their time on personal research and three per cent on graduate research and had the highest amount of 'unallocable' time (24 per cent). The position in social studies is that 21 per cent of time is allocated to personal research with a further three per cent on graduate research time. This suggests that a figure of 20 per cent is a reasonable proportion to take for the amount of time spent on educational research and development.

The next crucial figure is the salary. The salary scales were altered in October 1969. If one uses mid-points of the Lecturer scale as the likely median salary this suggests a figure of between £1,930 and £2,100—say £2,000. This assumes that the lower salaries of research assistants and research officers counter-balance the Professor and Reader salaries and leave the median salary at the £2,000 mark. It is possible to check this figure from Statistics of Education 1969, vol. 6. Here Departmental expenditure on salaries for 1968/9 is shown (Table 47) as is the number of staff in Departments as at December 31st, 1969 (Table 38). The results are remarkable. The mean salary for Education departments is about £1,680 and in social studies Departments it is £2,200. A mean salary of £2,000 now seems a little dubious, but one must remember that much research work is carried out in Departments other than Education.

If one accepts a mean salary of £2,000, a total education staff of 1,400 for England and Wales (Table 38) then the total salary expenditure is £2·8m, 20 per cent of which gives a figure of £560,000. Again, a simple check reveals some discrepancies. Total Departmental expenditure on full-time teaching and research staff in 1968/69 in Departments of Education was £2·35m in England and Wales (Table 47) and 20 per cent of this figure is £470,000. This could be explained by the extra staff that would have been recruited as from September 1969 and which would not of course be reflected in the 1968/9 salary expenditure. One can perhaps suggest a compromise figure of about £500,000 for 1968/9 and £600,000 for 1969/70. To this could be added some notional figure of the research work carried out in other Departments which seem to have higher mean salaries and a higher proportion of time devoted to research. There is no means of knowing what figure this might be and it is probably best to leave the problem unsolved. One can simply note that £500,000 and £600,000 are minimum figures for the educational research contribution of the Universities for 1968/9 and 1969/70. There are no data available on the position in the University Departments in 1971/2 and hence figures for this period have not been estimated.

The Colleges of Education and Colleges within the Further Education (FE) sector contribute negligible amounts to educational research. This is a disappointing, but not surprising, conclusion. No figures are available comparable with the UGC survey and hence it is not possible to put a figure on the contribution of staff time. Perhaps some more detailed inquiry will be conducted in the wake of the James Report but in the meantime casual evidence suggests that one must reluctantly agree that there is much justification for this assessment of the College contribution. Such evidence is available from the internal survey made by the Institute of Education, London, which indicates that only four of the associated Colleges are able to attract fundable projects. Apart from these, the research work takes the form of individual personal higher degree work, and some indication of the extent of this involvement is given by the fact that about 200 of the 2,000 or more staff of the London Institute Colleges have been awarded the title of recognized teacher of the University—a status which is normally accorded on the basis of evidence of research work within the candidate's subject. No College has a staff member whose appointment is concerned specifically with research, except for the Further Education Research Unit at Garnett College (Technical), where the appointment was made by the ILEA. Elsewhere, although some research inquiries are conducted by Colleges, the general conclusion is 'it would be far from true to say that staff engagement in research in the educational sciences is a major feature of College of Education life' (internal working document of Institute of Education, London). The London Institute and its associated Colleges is the largest Institute and is arguably the best equipped to conduct and encourage research in its Colleges. The picture elsewhere is therefore likely to be worse rather than better, and hence one can conclude that the research effort of Colleges is too small to be included.

One certainly hopes that this situation changes radically in the very near future. One of the main beneficiaries of educational research should surely be the teacher and it seems logical that teaching effectiveness can be improved through awareness and practice of research results. Clearly, this involves either direct involvement in research by the teacher personally, or a close acquaintance with research activity throughout his or her professional life. Such close acquaintance is most likely to be encouraged by a teacher education which utilizes research findings as part of course material. Clearly, this implies that College of Education staff should themselves be directly involved in educational research. It is also the view of some, like Michael Young (1965), discussed later, that educational research cannot be divorced from innovation in methods, and hence there is need for a more direct involvement with schools and Colleges. According to this view only by integrating research, innovation, and teaching practice by means of a lively College education and training together with regular in-service courses, can educational research and practice develop to their mutual benefit. The Colleges and the ATCDE are fully aware of the need for the participation of Colleges in educational research and development and by working through the ATCDE, UCET and similar bodies, it is hoped that funds and materials will be made available for the training of research staff and the involvement of Colleges in research activity.

Very little is known about educational research in FE. The NFER keeps a list of research titles of on-going studies in Further Education, but these are either small-scale inquiries, or more typically represent part-time higher degree work at universities. The recent Brunel FE Monographs (Cole and Van der Eyken, 1971) provide a survey of current research in FE, listing all on-going work. Much of this survey represents individual study for higher degrees and much of the resources therefore derive from personal time rather than college-based resources. The net effect of FE resources is therefore very small.

The reasons are not hard to discover: the pressure of student numbers; the irregular and fluctuating nature of courses; the disruption of teaching practice and industrial visits; and above all, the tradition noted by many (Robinson, 1968), that colleges are primarily teaching establishments and hence little time and few facilities are available for research work. One hopes that this position, too, is changing. The impact of research activity in polytechnics has been steady but significant, and no doubt will percolate through other FE colleges. As with colleges of education, it is to be hoped that the stimulus of research will make itself felt among both staff and students in colleges of FE.

Results

The results of this long process of collection and collation are shown in Tables 1.1 and 1.3. The totals for 1967/8, 1968/9 and 1969/70 are as complete as possible but naturally there are some incomplete records for 1970/1 and of course a number of omissions in 1971/2, where only the major bodies can forecast commitments for that year, and in any case new work may well be commissioned and start in that time period. The basis of the data is the project undertaken by the institution and therefore the distribution of resources shown in the tables is by institutions. Table 1.1 provides a summary of the projects and resources available in each of the five years, together with the estimate of staff time derived from the CVC data relating to education departments, which is discussed earlier.

Another point to consider is the value of expressing these figures in constant terms. The advantages of such a course are that over five years price changes will affect the values of appropriations and that it would be useful to estimate the trend in R & D funding over the period in real terms. In practice the difficulties are considerable and the benefits marginal. It is not easy to decide on a base year. 1967/8 is 'abnormal' in the sense that relatively few projects were funded in that year coming as it did towards the beginning of rapid expansion, and it could be misleading to base money values on this early period. 1969/70 or 1968/9 would be better but these years are aggregated for

TABLE 1.1: *Resources for educational R & D in England and Wales*

INSTITUTION	1967/8		1968/9		1969/70		1970/1		1971/2	
	Resources	Projects	Resources	Projects	Resources	Projects	Resources	Projects	Resources	Projects
Universities	682,600	139	1,238,000	202	1,523,900	250	1,447,000	253	1,271,000	171
Polytechnics	6,000	2	7,100	2	7,500	4	6,000	4	3,000	2
Colleges of Education	21,000	5	59,000	9	63,000	8	78,000	11	73,000	9
Other Institutions	321,200	43	443,800	66	482,000	78	496,000	70	437,500	42
Sub-total	1,030,800	189	1,747,900	279	2,076,400	340	2,027,000	328	1,784,500	224
Other resources—RNID, etc. RNIB	107,000		107,000		107,000		107,000		107,000	
University staff time	400,000		500,000		600,000		600,000		NA	
TOTAL	1,537,800		2,354,900		2,783,400		2,734,000		1,891,500	

the main analysis and it seemed odd to separate them for purposes of finding a base year. Neither is it easy to think of a price deflator. The index of retail prices is not really suitable; wages or earnings indices are better but do not catch all R & D costs, and hence must be suspect. Finally, there is the point that in most R & D contracts there are clauses which allow performers to claim for certain expenses under 'cost of living' clauses, for items such as salary awards.

Thus while one *can* distinguish between current and real prices it is not easy to decide on a base date or a deflator, nor to distinguish which cash flows should be subject to discounting. Hence the decision not to attempt the exercise. Most of the analysis centres on two years only and given the major difficulties and marginal benefits it was decided to leave all sums in current prices.

However it is interesting to note the effect of inflation (at a mild rate of four and a half per cent p.a.) on R & D grants and this is shown in Table 1.2. It can be seen that future sums from 1969/70 onwards are now much less imposing.

Nevertheless, the objections are strong and the benefits limited and the rest of the work is left in current prices.

The point should also be made that most independent institutions have an element of 'overheads' included in their R & D funds. This covers buildings, administration etc. which is not included in most university grant awards because they are already paid for by UGC funds. There are slight problems of comparability between the 'Independent' institutions and others because some part of their funds are not R & D funds but administrative costs incurred in R & D. The point is discussed again in another context in Chapter 3 but it should be noted here when viewing Tables 1.1 and 1.2.

There is nothing surprising in the results. They confirm the widely held view that most educational R & D work is carried out in

TABLE 1.2: *Recalculated version of table 1.1*

	1967/68	1968/69	1969/70	1970/71	1971/72
Universities . .	682,600	1,186,961	1,400,901	1,275,339	1,074,024
Polytechnics . .	6,000	6,807	6,895	5,288	2,535
Colleges of Education	21,000	56,568	57,915	68,747	61,687
Other Institutions .	321,200	425,503	443,096	437,158	369,697
Sub-total .	1,030,800	1,675,839	1,908,807	1,786,533	1,507,943
Other resources .	107,000	102,589	98,364	94,307	90,417
University staff . . .	400,000	479,386	551,572	528,821	N/A
Total . .	1,537,800	2,257,814	2,558,742	2,409,660	1,598,361

TABLE 1.3: *Some estimates of educational R & D expenditure*

Source			*Est. Ed. Research*[1]	*Total Ed. Exp.*[2]	% *(1) on* (2)
(1)	Dr Wall	1959	£100,000	£700 million	0·01%
(2)	Dr Wall	1968	£3,000,000	£1,800 million	0·16%
(3)	Dr Wall	1968	£500,000+	£1,800 million	0·02%
(4)	DES	1969	£2½–3 million	£1,852 million	0·13%
(5)	Prof. Taylor	1971	£3½ million	£2,000 million	0·17%

(1) *Educational Research and the Needs of the Schools* by W. D. Wall. Available from the National Association of Inspectors of Schools and Educational Organizers, 'Pencraig', Colwall Stone, Malvern, Worcestershire.

(2) *Educational Research in Britain* edited H. J. Butcher: University of London Press, 1968. Chapter 1 by Dr Wall.

(3) *Educational Research*, Vol. 10, No. 3: June, 1968.

(4) *Educational Research and Development in England and Wales*; the most comprehensive summary of educational research available to date, prepared by the Department of Education and Science for the OECD meeting in June, 1969.

(5) 'Alternative Futures in Education', *British Journal of Educational Technology*, No. 2, Vol. 2: May, 1971.

universities (70 to 75 per cent) and very little work is done in colleges of education (three per cent) or polytechnics (four per cent). Other institutions carry out a substantial amount of work and are analysed more fully in Chapter 3. It can be seen clearly here that most of the work is done by NFER and a few other independent institutions. The rest of 'other institutions' are comprised of a large number of institutions which vary enormously in size and importance from Schools Council and NCET to individual schools and private individuals. They are all engaged on one or two projects only and hence there is a long 'tail' of other institutions supporting the relatively large contribution made by NFER and a few other major institutions which fall in this category. The full list of 'other institutions' is given in Appendix 1.

Table 1.3 is a summary of previous attempts to estimate resources available for educational research, and this provides a perspective for the current figures. The size of the resources available also causes little surprise. They are about the same as, or perhaps a little less than previous estimates, and this is a little odd given the extensive coverage given to 'educational research' and to the wider range of sources which have been used. The total figures, however, are still disappointingly small and continue to justify the view that very little is spent on educational R & D compared with the total resources available for education. Taking the figure for educational R & D in 1968/9 of £2·35m this represents no more than 0·13 per cent of total current and capital educational expenditure in England and Wales which by most available criteria seems too small. This problem is developed more fully later. It makes a considerable difference to the results if alternative figures are used for computing sums like these as Table 1.4 shows. Total current *and* capital expenditures for England and Wales in 1968/9 were £1,850m (but £1,540m for current expenditure only) (Statistics of Education, Vol. 5, 1971). If the larger figure is taken then Educational R & D in that year is only 0·13 per cent. If the *UK* expenditure figures are taken then some further adjustments are necessary. Educational R & D must now be increased to include the Scottish Council for Educational Research (£42,000, 1968/9) and the work of the Northern Ireland Council for Educational Research (£5,000, 1969). These figures are taken from the Reports and from the Council of Europe survey of educational research, 1971. They are not computed in the same way as those for England and Wales but the differences are probably not significant. The Scottish and Irish Universities contribute about £218,000 using the same methods and figures drawn from the CVC data, and to this must be added sponsored work for SSRC and elsewhere. The total amount is thus about £300,000 which suggests a UK figure for Educational R & D of some £2·65m in 1968/9. The latest figures for *UK* educational expenditure are those for 1968/9 and are £1,780m for *current* expenditure and £2,157m for *current and capital* expenditure. The percentage figures are therefore 0·15 per cent and 0·12

TABLE 1.4: *Educational R & D in 1968/9 and educational expenditure*

Educational R & D in England and Wales as percentage of current expenditure on Education in England and Wales	0·15%
Educational R & D in England and Wales as percentage of current and capital expenditure on Education in England and Wales .	0·13%
Educational R & D in UK as percentage of current expenditure on Education in UK	0·15%
Educational R & D in UK as percentage of current and capital expenditure on Education in UK	0·12%

Notes: Year 1968/9
Educational R & D in England and Wales = £2·35 m.
Educational R & D in UK = £2·65 m.
Total current expenditure on Education in England and Wales = £1,540 m.
Total current and capital expenditure on Education in England and Wales = £1,850 m.
Total current expenditure on Education in UK = £1,780 m.
Total current and capital expenditure on Education in UK = £2,157 m.

Statistics of Expenditure from: *Statistics of Education*, Vol. 5, HMSO, 1971.
Statistics of Education in the UK, HMSO, 1971.

per cent respectively. It can be seen clearly that the selective use of the figures can be misleading and hence 'the amount we spend on educational R & D' can range between £2·35m and £2·65m and between 0·12 per cent and 0·15 per cent of 'total educational expenditure' in 1968/9. The later years can be calculated in a similar fashion if one is prepared to estimate the expenditure figures for Scotland and Northern Ireland.

The conclusion, then, is that about £2m p.a. is available for educational R & D from external funds during the period 1968–70 and that inclusive of the Universities' research efforts, the total available is about £2½m, which represents about 0·13 per cent of total *current and capital* educational expenditure in England and Wales. This is not a remarkable conclusion although even given the very wide coverage of R & D projects taken it is still somewhat lower than other estimates might suggest. The interest and value of this survey, however, lies primarily in the analysis of these aggregate figures and the following chapters provide more detailed consideration of how these funds are allocated between subject areas and sectors of education.

CHAPTER 2

The Distribution of Resources

The distribution of funds in 1968/9, 1969/70 subject is shown in Table 2.1. It was felt that the financial years of 1968/70 would be the years for which information would be most complete and accurate and it also seemed that to analyse in detail a single year could be misleading because a large number of projects might happen to start or finish in that year. Hence, the years 1968/70 represent the maximum period for which information is both complete and accurate and a minimum period for which one would contemplate a detailed breakdown of the figures. It must always be remembered that the figures refer to the two-year period 1968/70 and hence although the financial figures are accurate, there is some double counting of projects. There are not 619 projects on-going in this period. There are

TABLE 2.1: *Resources for educational R & D by subject—1968–9/1969–70*

SUBJECT	*Projects*	%	*Resources*	%
General; Bibliography; History; Research, etc.	14	2·3	18,000	0·47
Economics; Planning; Finance	16	2·6	95,000	2·5
Architecture and Buildings	17	2·7	85,000	2·2
Administration; regulations	13	2·1	64,000	1·7
Schools—organization	16	2·6	113,000	2·9
Curriculum Studies	165	26·7	1,730,000	45·0
Psychology of Education—selection, assessment, evaluation, examinations	81	13·1	425,000	11·1
Psychology of Education—teaching, learning, ability, training	133	21·5	568,000	14·8
Sociology of Education	48	7·8	314,000	8·2
Academic profession including in-service and teacher training	28	4·5	114,000	3·0
Further Education	14	2·3	63,000	1·6
Higher Education	27	4·4	110,000	2·9
Counselling and VG	7	1·1	41,000	1·1
Education of mentally and physically handicapped	40	6·5	97,000	2·5
TOTAL	619	100·2	3,837,000	100·0

279 in 1968/9 and 340 in 1969/70—a total of 619, which, of course, is a double counting of most of the projects. It is not possible to identify which projects started, finished, or continued without individual counting. However, this is not a serious problem provided one remembers that the projects column is virtually double the actual number of on-going in those years. Also it can be noted that the totals do not sum accurately due to rounding errors.

The subject categories are open to much discussion. There is obviously a large number of possible classifications and categories for educational research ranging from the comprehensive indexing classification of the US Educational Resources Information Center (ERIC) and the education study areas index used by the National Register of Educational Researchers in the US to the much simpler classifications used by the Society for Research into Higher Education (SRHE) and the DES. The classification used needs to be small enough to be convenient, given that only about 500 projects are available and yet large enough to convey the distribution of projects between subject areas in reasonable detail.

The classification adopted is a hybrid form based on the DES classification which includes the peripheral areas of educational research such as architecture and buildings, administration, etc., and the SRHE Register which is a sound, simple listing of the traditional areas of the subject. In addition, it was felt that counselling and Vocational Guidance studies (VG) did not fit easily into any other category and also that it was useful to identify work in the field of the education of the mentally and physically handicapped. This latter category was particularly useful because much of the medical/educational orientated research work is carried out in this area.

The results of this collation and tabulation are interesting. As was expected, curriculum development studies dominate the field, taking over one-quarter of the projects and nearly half the finance. If both categories of psychology of education are summed they provide the second major group of studies, taking 35 per cent of the projects and 26 per cent of the funds. The two traditional areas of interest are very well entrenched indeed.

Other categories are more notable for the small size or share of resources. Further Education is seen again as the 'Cinderella' of research activity together with counselling and VG, which is in any case a relatively new area of inquiry. Educational administration seems surprisingly neglected considering the importance of the service in distributing and controlling the resources for education, although doubtless some of the projects included within the finance and economics of education are at least indirectly concerned with administration and policy formulation. Of the other categories, one notes the figures, but they occasion little surprise or comment.

This cannot be said of Table 2.2 which shows the allocation of funds and projects by sector of education. Many projects were concerned with problems of transfer from one sector to another, particularly in curriculum development where the age of primary/secondary transfer is so variable. This explains the insertion of transition categories between each of the five main categories of education. There is a final sector—the transition from education to employment—which has generated some studies recently.

It is not surprising that the secondary sector should take a larger share of resources than the other categories, but that it should secure 30 per cent of the projects and nearly 50 per cent of the funds represents a remarkable domination of educational research. If the 'transition' projects are re-allocated to the five main sectors the domination of the secondary sector becomes even more complete. The most likely explanation is the enormous growth of curriculum development and evaluation in the last decade. There are obviously more subjects in the secondary curriculum and hence there is scope for more work. The materials and equipment are also more expensive to test and develop and this presumably explains the difference between the figures for projects and the funds available in secondary education. The interest in and importance of Higher Education is a widely reported feature of the educational world, but it is still surprising to discover that the sector takes over one-quarter of the projects and 16 per cent of the funds for the research. It appears that the problems of Higher Education are regarded as more important for research purposes if not more important than the

TABLE 2.2: *Resources for educational R & D by sector of education 1968–9/1969–70*

SECTOR	*Projects*	%	*Resources*	%
Pre-school	4	0·06	33,000	0·86
Primary	87	14·1	476,000	12·4
Transition	55	8·9	357,000	9·3
Secondary	192	31·1	1,842,000	47·9
Transition	22	3·6	87,000	2·3
Further Education	33	5·3	144,000	3·7
Higher Education (incl. Coll. of Ed.) .	164	26·6	630,000	16·4
Transition from Education to Work .	9	1·5	22,000	0·57
The whole system	53	8·6	248,000	6·4
TOTAL	619	99·8	3,839,000	99·8

problems encountered in pre-school or primary education, perhaps because this sector yields problems which are more immediate to the researchers who are themselves in the sector. No doubt this reflects the impact of the Robbins Report and the rapid growth of student numbers in Higher Education, and the economic, social and educational problems associated with this growth. A number of studies are concerned with forecasting student numbers and the administrative and economic difficulties of financing the University and Polytechnics expansion so that accommodation and facilities keep pace with student enrolments. Nevertheless, the size of the research effort in relation to other sectors seems surprising.

Perhaps it is not that Higher Education is so large, but that pre-school and primary resources are so low that should cause surprise. This area is one which takes £520m or about 28 per cent of the total educational budget. It is an area well documented by Plowden and generally recognized as being a major determinant of subsequent success. The need seems to be for a major inquiry and evaluation and the assessment of the benefits and costs of pre-school and primary provision compared with other sectors of education. If there is an obvious hole or gap in our research efforts, it seems to be in primary and pre-school education. Even when the transition projects are re-allocated between pre-school and primary education the former takes only 1·5 per cent of the total and certainly this seems an area which needs far greater support in the future.

Further Education remains, as ever, the smallest single category. This is in sharp contrast to its status as the fastest growing category as reflected in student numbers, together with Colleges of Education, and hence it would seem that the most rapidly developing area is one which we know least. The range of work carried out by Colleges of FE is bewildering in its range, level, and student support and we know surprisingly little about either the costs, or the effectiveness of the Colleges. Apart from the FE Unit at Brunel, very little systematic work is on-going in this sector. The 'Transition from Education to Work' sector is also disappointingly thin. It is increasingly the case that young people find themselves in great difficulty when forced to seek employment at the age 15–18. The difficulties are of several kinds—the economic problems of finding work at all; the vocational, personal, and perhaps psychological problems of choosing satisfying work; and of course the rather bewildering choice between work and one of the many FE and HE courses available. Little is known about how to guide and counsel young children and this must cause great losses to both the individuals and the community.

Finally, something should be said on the sector concerned with the educational system as a whole. Clearly, some research projects were concerned with education as an activity, or with basic research into learning which would have application over the whole system—hence the need for this category. Much work on techniques, such as programmed learning and teaching machines, and administrative changes are included in this category and some of the work on mentally and physically handicapped children can be allocated to this sector because it is appropriate to children of all ages, although where it is specific to young children or to adolescents in training, then it has been allocated accordingly. Educational Technology is a difficult subject to categorize: much research is conducted by psychologists, some by engineers, and teachers in schools, universities, and particularly the armed services. It was not thought necessary to have a separate category for the topic because so much is part of 'psychology'. A full account of current work is available from NCET and their bibliography of research work (Erault & Squires, 1971).

Allocation between basic research and development

Few topics generate more discussion, confusion and disagreement than the distinctions between different types of research and development. The purpose of the present discussion is to point out existing views, to indicate why discussion of the distinctions is important, and finally to indicate the definitions used in the present study and to comment briefly on the results. The literature provides several definitions and distinctions: 'The objective of research activities are to discover, reinforce, or refine knowledge. Research is carried out because we want to know something . . . or because we want to establish the direction or nature of so-called cost and effective interactions.' 'The objectives of development activities carried out in the field of education are to produce materials, techniques, processes, hardware, and organizational formats for instruction' ('Educational Research and Development in the US,' OECD, 1969).

A second view provides the following definition: Fundamental research can be seen as 'directed to the development and testing of a coherent body of theory in its own field and to the fashioning of the appropriate instruments of study and measurement'. Development, however, is seen as 'concerned principally with an immediate complex practical problem' (Wall, 1962).

The definitions above distinguish between research and development by the purposes for which the project is undertaken. Other commentators have attacked the problem by making distinctions based on the audience, thus 'basic research is that which is carried out by a scientist who hopes his findings will be principally of interest to his scientific colleagues, while applied research is intended to produce findings which will be of greater interest to the investigator's employer and to the lay public' (Storer, 1966).

Others have pointed, not to the topics of study nor the motives of the investigators, but the conditions under which the studies are made. They indicate a distinction between decision-orientated study in which '. . . the investigator is asked to provide information wanted by a decision-maker . . . the decision-orientated study is a commissioned study'. This is contrasted with '. . . the conclusion-orientated study on the other hand takes its direction from the investigator, commitments and hunches. The aim is to conceptualize and understand the chosen phenomenon' (Cronbach and Suppes, 1969). This kind of distinction seems to have been ignored by the DES and Ministry of Technology. In compiling the statistics of science and technology, the definitions taken are: *basic research*—work undertaken for the advancement of knowledge without specific commercial objectives; *applied research*—research undertaken with either a general or a particular commercial objective in view; *development*—research directed to the introduction or improvement of specific projects or operations up to and including the prototype or pilot plant stage. (Statistics of Science and Technology, Great Britain, DES and Ministry of Technology, 1970.)

The DES (Great Britain, DES, 1970) have found other distinctions useful, and in their output budgeting study and the inquiry into the economic benefits of basic scientific research (Byatt and Cohen, 1969), R & D is classified in terms of the purposes and conditions of the work undertaken. Thus, *curiosity-orientated research* has no definite goals and no prospects of development or applications which may yield benefits. Some projects do, of course, lead to major benefits in the long run, but the work is financed and conducted on the general understanding that no benefits, other than the advancement of knowledge, are expected. *Mission-orientated research* is related to projects where there is scope for future application and a general expectation that benefits will accrue to society and the economy in the medium term. One suspects that much educational and medical research falls into this category. *Action-orientated research* is intended to have a specific application in a field of activity where it will lead to some definite benefit, or output other than the advancement of knowledge. *Development* is taken to be the application of results and the production of prototypes, materials, piloting of procedures and operations (DES, 1970, pp. 61–3).

All, or most of these distinctions are useful providing the categories are not too sharply demarcated, but this view is sharply challenged by Reagan (1967) who asks whether the discussion has any real value because policy and practice, the guidance of which is the main purpose of the discussion over definitions, seems to vary almost as much as the theorizing. In short, the semantic debate seems to contribute little in the assistance of policy decisions.

The distinction between basic research and development is far from academic and assistance in policy-making is only one of several areas where it is important to establish criteria for distinguishing between two or more activities. It is a minor point but one must recognize that a higher prestige and status is accorded by academics and, perhaps, the public, to basic research work compared with development work. In itself this is relatively unimportant, but it can have important effects upon the recruitment and retention of good research workers. It has sometimes been argued that distinctions like this account for the relative neglect of engineering compared with the natural sciences like physics and chemistry, and hence one must recognize the pervasive influence of an image or a status accorded to one type of activity compared with another.

Nevertheless, the main reason for making distinctions lies in the determination of policy and the effects of policy of both sponsors and the institutions which carry out work. If an institution has a policy of conducting applied or development or basic work, then clearly it is important that some definition be made and be generally accepted so that as new projects arise, they can be rejected or modified if they fall outside the policy boundaries. This need not imply a rigid unchanging policy, but simply provide guidelines for the acceptance or rejection of new projects. If the nature of the work changes, then clearly policy decisions to embrace the new kind of work must be taken and once more, therefore, the question of definition arises. It is perhaps more important that sponsors are clear on this matter of definition. A number of sponsoring bodies have 'policies' which involve either a preference for basic or development work, which may be of varying strengths or a clear-cut commitment to one to the exclusion of the other. Given this, it is clear that distinctions between projects which are before the appropriate committee for funding must be made at least in part upon the definitions of basic and applied research. It is possible to draft and re-draft grant applications so that they seem to comply more closely with the requirements of the sponsors' policy on, say, basic research, but if definitions and meanings were made clear, much confusion and disappointment could be avoided.

There is no need to prolong the discussion—it has been sufficient to show only that opinions vary, which is obvious enough, but also to demonstrate that these differences can have important consequences.

The definitions adopted here are those of the US Office of Education (OECD, 1969). Thus, development is defined as the 'production of materials, techniques, processes, hardware and organizational formats for instruction'. All other types of research are considered to be 'research'. This leaves considerable scope for further distinctions within this category, applied research, action-orientated research, etc., but it was decided that a simple two-way division was more appropriate. Few problems arose in the actual allocation of the projects into two categories and the only major difficulty was the allocation of some test development projects. Clearly, the tests are applied to measure achievement, attitudes, etc., and hence clearly fall within the category of 'techniques for instruction'. On the other hand, devising and validating tests is an important part of research work and falls within the framework of devising instruments for study. It was finally decided that the construction of tests was research but the application of tests in the course of, say, a curriculum development study, was development.

The results are shown in Table 2.3. It is sometimes argued that the balance of educational R & D funds tends to favour development rather than basic research. At first sight this seems to be incorrect—roughly half the projects and finance are available for basic research. As indicated above, however, development has been somewhat narrowly defined leaving research as the residual item into which has been placed all basic, applied, action, and problem-orientated work, including many surveys which are perhaps more accurately described as inquiries. Hence, too much should not be made of the figures. It seems possible, from the data, that development work is more expensive per project than basic research. If one assumes that the number of projects is exactly double counted—i.e. that there are 177 research projects and 132 development projects, then the cost per project is £9,500 for research and £16,240 for development. This is readily explained by the expense of curriculum materials, preparation of instruments, hardware, etc. No figures are available as to the relative proportions of researchers, but one suspects that development projects require more workers in the field than most basic research work. It seems that development in the social sciences and education follows the pattern of the natural sciences where basic research is fairly inexpensive, but development costs are very high—

TABLE 2.3: *Resources for educational R & D by type of research—1968–9/1969–70*

DEVELOPMENT		RESEARCH	%	DEVELOPMENT	%	TOTAL
Projects		354	57·0	265	43·0	619
Resources	£	1,682,000	44·0	2,152,000	56·0	3,834,000

by a factor of at least 10 according to Rothschild (Rothschild Report, Great Britain, 1971, p. 5). It is also the view of Rothschild that development work should have a probability of success of at least 0·9 before work is undertaken. This is very high indeed and most educational development projects would find it difficult to guarantee that level of certainty.

However, the difficult problem in education is basic research and it is almost impossible to isolate how many projects and how much resources are allocated to this area without undertaking a re-sort for all projects. One would like to do this but the constraints are severe—one can only make an informed guess that perhaps 15 per cent of projects and less than 10 per cent of funds are devoted to what Wall would define as basic research.

CHAPTER 3

The Sponsors of Educational Research and Development

The sources of finance for educational research are shown in Table 3.1. The results are unremarkable, but they do clarify the generally accepted position. The big three or four are obviously the Schools Council, DES, Nuffield, and SSRC, which provide about 85 per cent of the total funds available. 'Other institutions' are detailed in Appendix 2. Once more one should remember that figures refer to the two-year period 1968–70.

The compilation of this table involved several problems. Clearly, NFER is a body which both carries out research for sponsors and finances its own work. It has proved a little difficult to separate the resources for every project undertaken by NFER since 1967/8 so as to apportion resources accurately between Tables 1.1 and 3.1. Another problem is the double counting of projects which are financed by two or three bodies. It is not uncommon for DES or other sponsors to supplement or finance work providing the institution itself offers a contribution: and hence the task of identifying a sponsor and the appropriate sums involved becomes very difficult. This is particularly true in the case of DES which not only carries out its own research but sponsors work and commissions work on behalf of other bodies. The situation is now (1971) clarified in that the

TABLE 3.1: *Sources of finance for educational research—1968–9/1969–70*

SOURCE	£	%	NO. OF PROJECTS	%
Schools Council	1,218,000	31·7	134	21·6
DES	928,000	24·1	210	33·8
Nuffield Foundation	784,000	20·4	50	8·1
SSRC	306,000	8·0	104	16·7
Leverhulme	174,000	4·5	53	8·5
NFER	145,000	3·8	14	2·3
Ford	79,000	2·1	13	2·1
Other	209,000	5·4	44	7·1
	3,843,000	100·0	623	100·2

Schools Council have, since April 1970, been responsible for all of their budget, rather than commissioning £100,000 of work (roughly one-fifth of the annual research budget) through the DES. The projects commissioned by DES are shown in their quarterly survey of research work where it is made fairly clear which projects are their own and which are commissioned on behalf of the Schools Council. However, it may be that some double counting has occurred, although the intention is that the DES figure should include about £100,000 of Schools Council money. Also included in the DES total is the finance made available to the Committee for Research and Development in Modern Languages (CRDML) which was attached to the Committee for Instruction in Language Teaching (CILT) and recommended research work in appropriate fields to the DES which supported some (but not others) from the funds available. CRDML was disbanded in September 1970. In dealing with these funds one came across the familiar difficulty of what is 'educational' as distinguished from the subject area—in this case Linguistics. The opinion of CILT was consulted and agreement reached as to the projects falling within linguistics, and those falling into the category of educational research. The DES also commissioned work—and still does on behalf of NCET and this too is reflected in the figures.

The figure for the Nuffield Foundation looks a little high compared with the £300,000+ each year indicated in their annual report. This is primarily due to the fact that some medical/educational projects have been included and that the 'allocated' expenditure has been more than the actual expenditure.

A similar problem exists between Schools Council and Nuffield over the language and science projects. Some projects were started by Nuffield and taken over by Schools Council; others have had supplementary grants from either or both bodies and others have evaluation studies grafted on to them by DES carried out by NFER or a University. It can be very confusing. Where projects have been jointly financed, e.g. International Association for the Evaluation of Achievement (IEA), then the appropriate figures have been recorded under the sponsors involved. This means double counting the projects and hence the tables have been corrected. Nevertheless, comparison of Tables 1.1 and 3.1 does reveal some minor discrepancies which are due to rounding errors and the difficulty of making all the necessary corrections and adjustments.

It should be stressed once more at this point that the figures recorded here refer to educational R & D only and two points therefore need discussion—student grants and overheads.

The expenditure made by the sponsoring bodies towards grants to students/researchers for Fellowships, travel, fees, and/or maintenance have not been included. There is a case for inclusion—research work is performed by post-graduate students and some assistance is available for researchers including those working in Education. However, the difficulty of separating research degrees from research as part of a degree course requirements and the large number of small sums for travel, etc., prevented full account of this area from being recorded.

The problem is most acute in SSRC and Leverhulme, and Ford. One of the main functions of the SSRC is to support research students. The number of post-graduate students in Education who receive grants is relatively small and it is doubtful if either the number of projects, or the quantity of money involved could affect appreciably the contribution of SSRC to educational research, but nevertheless funds are granted—although following the views expressed in Chapter 1, students grants are not included here.

The same comments are readily applicable to Leverhulme. Here, many small sums are advanced as Fellowships and studentships to individual students and researchers as a deliberate policy of the Trust Fund. These have not been considered to be research expenditure and only expenditure on projects (rather than individuals) has been included. In this sense the figures given for the sponsoring bodies may deviate from recorded expenditure in their accounts but in most cases the figures have been agreed with the bodies before publication.

Overheads are a more serious problem. Expense incurred in an organization such as the Schools Council, SSRC, NFER, etc. is substantial. Clearly, the functions of these bodies cannot be effectively pursued without an administrative machine and supporting staff such as librarians, statisticians, and information services. The familiar problem of what constitutes research expenditure is present again. The figures for NFER are collated from project expenditure which includes all overheads and service on-costs. A similar, though not identical, approach is adopted by the NCB. If grant-giving bodies did not have an administrative machine then grants could not be allocated efficiently. In this sense, therefore, the overheads of an organization are part of 'research-related' or 'overheads' expenditure and could be (should be?) included in the total figure along with university research time.

The sums involved, if this view is accepted, are impressive: the Schools Council organizations cost about £400,000 or nearly 40 per cent of the total budget; and NFER £150,000 or nearly 35 per cent of the budget. The DES figure cannot be ascertained and the reason indicates the objections to this approach—most organizations operate in areas other than educational research allocation and hence the apportionment of the administrative expenses becomes very difficult. Similarly, it is almost impossible to discover how much time and office/building expenses are incurred by SSRC, Nuffield, Leverhulme, etc. in the allocation of educational research grants. However, if one were to include these figures, the resources for educational research now would increase by perhaps another £1m.

It is useful to make the familiar point that if the research grants/ organizational overhead costs are of the order 70/30 or 60/40, then efficiency savings in organization of the order of, say five per cent make available sizeable sums for research. Administration is of course a necessary component of effective completion of research work, and no doubt Trust funds, Foundations, etc. are run as efficiently as possible, but if every £2,500 saved could be seen as representing an extra research officer to some project, then perhaps more effective use of the resources for educational research could be ensured.

Criteria for grant allocation

One of the most interesting parts of this project was the attempt to obtain a statement of the principles adopted by sponsors in allocating their funds. In fact, this proved unsuccessful, partly because sponsors simply drew our attention to 'policy statements' in the annual reports, and partly through a simple avoidance of the problem. It rapidly became apparent that no detailed inquiry into the decision-making process was possible and one can appreciate the problems faced by sponsors who perhaps wish to be as flexible as possible in the allocation of their funds. One is therefore left to cull the relevant policy and criteria statements from reports. This still makes an interesting exercise.

There is substantial uniformity of approach amongst most sponsors, both in the criteria adopted for selecting projects, and in the machinery for dealing with applications. The latter point is dealt with first. All requests for assistance are usually channelled through a series of committees which separate the possibles and probables from the rest. The important decision to support a particular project is taken by a panel of advisors who are usually regarded as expert, eminent people in the field. The final decision is taken (or ratified) by the trustees themselves on the recommendation of their advisory panel.

This pattern of initial selection, committee of experts, and final Board approval is fairly uniform across all sponsors, although clearly the larger the organization, the more extensive the committee system becomes. The organizational arrangements of the main sponsors will doubtless be familiar to most researchers, but familiarity is often not enough. It would be most useful if a short research directory were available which provided organizational charts giving details of the committee structure, members, and the machinery for dealing with applications for all the main sponsoring bodies. The need to meet the requirements of several committees, particularly when a project falls between disciplinary interests, can be most time-consuming. Thus, a project concerned with, say, primary schools and requiring sponsorship by DES will need to satisfy Planning Branch which handles almost all research proposals sponsored by DES; it must also satisfy Statistics if the project involves the collection and use of data of interest to Statistics Branch; and finally, Schools Branches 1 and 2 will probably be involved in the consultations. The file will then probably be sent to one or more of the HMIs, perhaps the educational research consultant, and finally sent to one of the senior administrative staff within the DES for a final decision. This process, with variations, is followed by the other large sponsors although the committee system adopted by Schools Council and SSRC allows the progress of the project to be followed more closely. In the event of a rejection, it is sometimes possible to locate the group which took the decision and to guess the reasons for the rejection. In the DES, the process of consultation adopted to decide the fate of research applications has the effect of obscuring the location and perhaps the reason for the success or failure of the projects. However, the machinery of decision making is fairly uniform: it is the criteria for decision making which constitute the important and interesting problem.

It is important to distinguish the policy guidelines provided by the terms of the Trust or the terms of reference of the Council from the allocation criteria adopted by advisory bodies/committees when projects reach them. The first category will allow an early rejection of all projects which do not fall within the area of the Foundation's interest. Thus, the Carnegie (UK) Trust does not support educational research at all although some of its interest in music, drama, visual arts, and the environment can be called 'educational'. Similarly,the Van Leer Foundation do support educational R & D, but they have quite strict policy guidelines which channel all resources into projects concerned with the education of socially and culturally disadvantaged children. Hence, work on higher education or design of school equipment or curriculum development would almost certainly not be supported by Van Leer, under the present terms of the Trust fund. Similarly, the guidelines established by some Trusts prohibit grants for buildings or for facilities as in the case of Leverhulme, or may deliberately encourage such provision as does the Wolfson Foundation. Even when the terms of the Trust are very loosely defined, the Trustees themselves may establish areas of interest and this creates broad guidelines which allow the initial selection and rejection of applications. These are frequently laid out in their reports and the following section briefly abstracts the main items culled from these official sources. They are available in most libraries but the extracts given here may be useful. The chapter ends with some more general remarks about the policy criteria of sponsoring bodies.

Leverhulme Trust

This was established in 1925 on the death of the first Viscount Lever and the income was to be used 'for the provision of scholarships for such purposes as research and education . . . as they, the trustees, may decide'. The general policy of the trustees has changed considerably since the 1930s as the need for 'scholarships' has declined with widespread State provision and as the income of the Trust has expanded (from £15,000 1925 to £950,000 1970). Policy may be summarized as follows:

(1) The trust deeds prevent grants for land, buildings and capital equipment.

(2) It is not policy to give programme grants. 'The normal duration of a grant seldom exceeds five years and most are for three years or under.'

(3) 'There are no limitations on the field of study which the trustees are prepared to support.' However, although no area of study is precluded, in practice awards are usually made within four categories—social studies including welfare and education, medical research, the natural sciences, and the humanities. It is relatively rare to find grants awarded to engineering and the applied sciences, fine arts, libraries, rural sciences, etc.

(4) 'There is no limit geographically to the distribution of support from the Leverhulme Trust.' Most grants go to institutions and individuals operating within the UK, but about 25 per cent tend to be awarded to those operating overseas.

(5) The trustees have, in the past, allocated resources in responses to application . . . 'since in general applications are a reasonable guide to where need is greatest and where interest in the subject of study is strongest'. Recently, however, grants have been made following an initiative taken by the trustees . . . 'in fields in which they feel further research is especially necessary, e.g. industrial relations, use of manpower resources and some of the fine arts'.

(6) The Trust takes the view that their role is to act as a supplement to public funds provided by State agencies. They have therefore

identified six categories within which they feel the project should be supported. A short quotation from the Sixth Report identifies these categories and it is unlikely that they will be changed for a number of years.

'There are, firstly, those projects for which channels of public support do not exist; the list of grants and fellowships recommended by the Trustees' Research Award Advisory Committee bears ample testimony to their existence. Secondly, many applications to the Trust are for relatively small amounts and tend to fall below the levels at which State agencies tend to work. Thirdly, there are also those projects of an experimental nature which require testing and proving before becoming established and supported from public funds; trusts and foundations are often able to accept a greater degree of risk than can the State. Fourthly, there are also projects where it may be advantageous, from the point of view of confidence in the results, to have certain projects financed from completely independent and objective sources; it is not insignificant that this view is accepted by Government itself and three, at least, of the Trustees' recent commitments overseas have been undertaken at the request of the Government in order that the study may be seen to be objective. Fifthly, there are projects where financial support from private sources may give greater flexibility in scope, organization and timing than those financed from public funds; this is often an attraction to voluntary organizations whose sources of income, dependent on voluntary subscription, are less secure or regular than those dependent on the tax payer. Finally, there is the great importance of having more than one source from which help may be sought. Mistakes or misjudgements are possible in the assessment of the value of individual projects; some projects may even fail to find support for reasons of prejudice or bias; others may wither through lack of encouragement, conscious or unconscious, and a multiplicity of sources provides a safety net for exceptional and worthwhile ideas which may, for various reasons, fail to find favour elsewhere.'

DES

No official policy has been provided by the DES and there is nothing in the DES annual reports to indicate the criteria by which research work is supported. The clearest recent statement of policy towards research available is the speech made by the Secretary of State for Education (Mrs Thatcher) at the Annual Members' Conference of the NFER in December 1970. After tracing the rise and decline of the research and development unit at the DES during the 1960s, she noted that it was established to increase the body of knowledge, to encourage a rise in the number of experienced research workers, and to establish educational research work at Universities and elsewhere. She then pointed to the disappointingly few conclusions in the vast efforts in which so many people are engaged at such great expense during that time. A clue to the new policy is then indicated by her comments that 'we have added to our problem by trying to investigate large, diffuse questions which were not susceptible of precise answers which might be of use to us'. She then argued that the Department's policy 'had to move from a basis of patronage to a basis of commission'. She continued 'this meant the active initiation of work by the Department on problems of its own choosing within a procedure and timetable which were relevant to its needs'. The broad criteria are then that projects should: (i) be of direct benefit to current (or immediate future) events, and/or (ii) be directed to solving or aiding decision making.

In a policy of commission there is the implied action of deliberately cultivating or directing research work in a particular area of concern to the decision makers. Once the research has been commissioned and absorbed by the Department, and once the decision has been taken, resources will then be switched elsewhere. Of course, events may move faster than anticipated and the decision may well be taken without regard to the results of the commissioned research. In either event, time is pressing and if policy or staffing constraints prevent external research being commissioned there is every reason to suppose that the work would be carried out internally. This has several consequences discussed later.

The Schools Council

The object of the Schools Council is revealed clearly in the Constitution. It 'shall be the promotion of education by carrying out research into and keeping under review the curricula, teaching methods, and examinations in schools including the organizations of schools so far as it affects their curricula' (Appendix B to the Council's 1969/70 Annual Report). To pursue this object the Council has powers to grant research funds. There appear to be few limits to their powers because the Council is able to:

(1) finance or assist anybody undertaking R & D work;
(2) offer advice to anybody;
(3) publish or assist in the preparation and publication of any work relating to the Council's activities;
(4) purchase, lease, or otherwise deal in property and materials, etc;
(5) 'do all such other lawful acts and things as are incidental to and necessary for the attainment of its object.'

The Schools Council therefore has a wide brief in the allocation of its R & D funds. Research funds gradually became available during the early years from about 1966–8 and as part of the adoption of the new Constitution in December 1968, various reviews of the Council's policy were undertaken. The Programme Committee became the major educational policy committee and the interesting point is that some attention was paid to research policy. A major area for the Council's interest was examinations and particularly the problems of comparability and cross-moderation between the Boards and between CSE and GCE. The other area is also discernible at this stage—'the need for a more positive programme designed to communicate to teachers' centres and individual teachers the progress of the Council's work and information about curriculum research and development generally' (Report 1968/9, p. 8). To this end the Council introduced *Dialogue* and there seemed to be some intention of establishing a national curriculum library and information service and some increase in the publications programme. It was also made clear at this point that 'fundamental research was not the Council's direct concern although there might be occasions when it should commission long-term research on matters bearing upon the curriculum' (p. 9). These three main points have remained unchanged since 1968. There has clearly been a considerable growth in the resources devoted to R & D and certainly the organization necessary to finance and monitor projects has become refined and there have been some attempts to re-consider the research policy. The clearest statement of research policy is that prepared by Professor J. Wrigley (Butcher and Pont [Eds.], 1970), which has remained almost unaltered through to the Eastbourne Conference, 1971. The major point is that for purposes of obtaining funds a project must satisfy three conditions. It must:

(1) be concerned with some aspect of curriculum development or examinations;
(2) be directly concerned with the improvement of the practice and technique of teaching in schools;
(3) 'fit into the overall policy of the Council'.

One other point made clear in Wrigley's account (1970) is that '. . . the Council is not a grant-giving body to those who seek finance to implement their own ideas for fundamental research'. For such people the SSRC or DES are available.

These points make the criteria for allocating research funds reasonably clear although there are two associated problems. The first is the relationship between curriculum development and research, and the second problem is the group of activities which can be placed under the heading of dissemination, utilization and feed-back.

The first point is treated well by Wrigley. It is readily admitted that there is not a clear-cut distinction between the two activities of curriculum development and research. While it is true that a development project usually produces some tangible benefit in the form of materials, etc., changes in curriculum usually require associated changes in teaching practice and any examination of changes in aims, objectives and teaching practice, and the subsequent effect on pupils' performance and attitudes could reasonably be considered research work. If nothing else, curriculum development is usually (or ought to be) evaluated in the school and classroom and this, too, is a form of research work. The relations between curriculum development and research therefore are very close and Wrigley makes the point very clear. 'It is also my view that in the long run fundamentals cannot be ignored, hence my concern for fundamental research and for better in-service and pre-service training of teachers' (p. 32). Indeed, this is put more forcibly at the Schools Council Conference in 1971 where, although (because of the shortage of funds) basic research was not contemplated, the point was made strongly that the time may soon come when the Council may have to devote more effort to the studies of basic educational problems.

The second point relates to the Council's concern for dissemination, utilization, diffusion and feed-back. It is true to say that some concern has been expressed about the diffusion of innovations and much attention will be paid in this report to the poor information channels which exist between performer, sponsor, and user. The Schools Council are well aware of this and confirmed at the Eastbourne Conference (1971) that extensions of existing projects for in-service training and dissemination by projects should take priority over proposals for new starts. Dissemination ranked second only to examinations research in the Council's priorities. Only lack of resources prevented the establishment of regional information centres and the idea of the information 'hive' which has been suggested for some time. *Dialogue*, however, was increased in size and was to be further improved as a major information channel.

Social Science Research Council

The educational research board of the SSRC first met in June 1966 and formed an integral part of the Council although it had 'the necessary autonomy to give expression to the special needs of research into education' (SSRC Annual Report, 1969/70, p. 38). The general objectives of SSRC derive from the recommendations of the Heyworth Committee on social studies and the chief objectives are:

(1) to encourage and support research in the social sciences;

(2) to provide and operate services for common use in carrying on such research;

(3) to arrange for post-graduate training in the social sciences;

(4) to provide advice and to disseminate knowledge on the social sciences.

From the very start it has been fairly clear that the SSRC's grants are 'primarily intended to provide initial support for new ideas and projects, particularly those whose applications may be valuable or which make a new contribution to theory or method' (SSRC Report, 1968, p. 5). There are fairly stringent conditions attached to the grants intended to make sure that the grant covers research only. Thus, SSRC does not advance funds towards publication or for conferences, nor do they grant funds for building, equipments, or other 'overheads' associated with the project. There is, however, a special allowance paid for independent research establishments not otherwise aided by the UGC. In effect, therefore, SSRC funds pay salaries and the direct travel and subsistence expenses incurred by the research work. The main criterion, then, in granting funds was the quality of the research proposal. By 1968/9 the SSRC was becoming actively concerned about the way in which grants were allocated. As their 1968/9 Report puts it, although in the early years the Council's approach was 'producer-orientated' guided largely by the existing academic interests of applicants, there was also the 'problem of identifying what are the most pressing research and training needs however these are defined' (p. 11). After some internal debate within the Council, they developed a number of instruments of research management—the prompted research project application, the programme research grant, the straightforward research contract, and finally the research unit. There was also some considerable interest in the idea of over-views by the research boards as a means of determining policies and priorities. This was duly undertaken in 1970 and the reports appear in the SSRC Annual Report 1969/70. The educational research board made a number of points which seemed to affect the allocation criteria. In their view it is difficult and 'perhaps unwise' for the SSRC to draw up shopping lists of educational priorities, but on the other hand they see it as 'essential that research programmes should be instituted in strategic areas'. The board felt that they should determine certain priorities (teacher education and utilization; nursery and pre-school education; minorities and the evaluation of new approaches to education) and they would invite applications for work in this area. They thus achieved a dual criterion for grant allocation:

(1) satisfying SSRC perceived needs;
(2) 'a degree of choice on the part of potential researchers'.

If one may summarize then the SSRC as a central body is concerned with fundamental research and with applied work and sets fairly stringent conditions on the use of its grant. It is also amongst the first of the sponsors to consider seriously the problem of a passive versus a directive role in grant administration. The educational research board seems to have adopted a rather uneasy stance on the question. On the one hand they are not happy about an active directive role, but on the other hand they seem to be able and willing to determine priority areas and persuade researchers to work in them.

The Nuffield Foundation

The objects of the Foundation are clearly laid out on the front pages of every Annual Report. They are:

(1) The advancement of health . . . in particular . . . by medical research and teaching and by the organization and development of medical and health services;
(2) the advancement of social well-being . . . by scientific research and the organization, development, and improvement of technical and commercial education including the training of teachers and provision of scholarships and prizes;
(3) the care and comfort of the aged poor;
(4) the advancement of education;
(5) such other charitable purposes as shall be declared in writing:
 (a) by Lord Nuffeld in his lifetime
 (b) after his death by all the ordinary trustees and managing trustees.

It is clear that the Nuffield Foundation has a wide range of interests of which educational and educational research is one—albeit a very important one. To scan any of the reports makes one well aware of the range and importance of its interests. It is difficult to indicate the size and importance of education within the total grants awarded because a number of auxiliary funds are associated with the central Nuffield Foundation fund and grants are made both for research and for fellowships both within and without the UK. However, if one takes the figures of the Nuffield fund only, education as a category seems to take something less than about 20 per cent of the total funds, although in many other cases in their science and medical allocations many of the grants are concerned with the teaching of this work.

It is not clear how policy is determined within the Nuffield Foundation, but one may cull a number of pointers from the Introduction to their Reports. Thus, in the 1966/7 Report one notes that 'everyone appreciates that a Foundation support must be comparatively short-lived if new work is to be supported and that return to the original sponsors cannot regularly bring a renewal of support however heartrending the case may be. Sometimes a year or two of additional help is given to ease the transition or absorbtion of distinguished work; more often the onus of continuing what has been well begun must be left to others.' Nuffield seems to be following the traditional view that they should be concerned with the initiation and development of projects for relatively short periods. In the 1968 Report attention is paid to the informational requirements and the attempt to provide an over-view of the project area before decisions are made. 'Otherwise the Foundation will be unable to recognize the best among the many ideas which it hears about in one way or another.' It was further noted that greater efficiency was needed in mounting and operating projects in order to make effective use of its scarce funds. Some further attention was paid to alternative sources of finance and it was noted that there was some danger of overlap between UGC and the research councils in the support of some projects. 'There is some danger that everyone will compete in paying for the exciting things and leave it to everyone else to come along later and finance the duller follow-up.' There was also the problem of financing fellowships and scholarships and striking a balance between this work and research grants and similarly between the balance between UK and overseas work. So far as the education section is concerned, the Nuffield Foundation is probably best known for its work in curriculum studies—Nuffield Science, Nuffield Maths, and the Humanities Project, which is a joint Schools Council/Nuffield Project, are household words in educational circles. However, this work has now passed its peak so far as the Nuffield Foundation is concerned largely because it is seen as the Schools Council's province to develop this work. From 1968 the Foundation notes that 'the emphasis of the Foundation's educational programme is likely to fall increasingly on higher education during the coming years'. The decision was taken in part because changes in the secondary school curriculums are now having an impact on university work, and partly because the higher education sector is perhaps facing greater strain than most other parts of the system. Finances therefore have been awarded to Bath for a project on Statistics and to the Inter-University Biology Project, and a grant has been made to Cambridge for research into new teaching methods in applied maths. There is also new work on child development financed at

Cambridge although this in no way impairs the continued support of Nuffield Science at Chelsea and the other on-going work. In addition to these major projects, the Nuffield Foundation also gives a large number of individual fellowships and scholarships and, of course, has major work for which it is both sponsor and performer of which the Resources for Learning Project is perhaps the best known example.

Decision criteria

When one draws together the policy statements and administrative procedures adopted by sponsors, one is struck by the similarity of policy and procedure and the variation in policy outcomes. The machinery of application is fairly uniform: forms are completed for most sponsors which require the usual details of project design, staffing, and costs. In practice there are variations—a much more formal approach is needed for SSRC submissions than, say, Leverhulme where a looser (but not less rigorous) submission procedure exists. In almost all cases it is common practice to discuss a proposed project with the officials of the sponsor and this gives some guide to the probability of success and the format for submission.

The next stage varies considerably in detail although the principle is uniform: applications are considered by a committee of experts/advisors. In the DES this is represented by 'internal consultations'. The Schools Council operate a 'round one' system where most of the interested subject committees consider the value of the work and the researchers are sometimes called in to answer queries. At SSRC the subject committee considers proposals and all large scale (in excess of £50,000) projects go forward to the full council for approval. Nuffield and Leverhulme simply take advice from experts and the Trustees make decisions on that advice.

The final stage represents senior administrative decisions at DES, a full council meeting after 'round two' at Schools Council, or the full meetings of other sponsors. In principle the machinery is simple: a careful separation of possibles, probables, and rejects, followed by more careful evaluation of probables only and a final choice.

Naturally, one now wishes to consider how decisions are actually made for the allocation of funds. The short answer is that, owing to the confidentiality of most policy meetings, there is no firm evidence available. One thus assumes that the decision making process is characterized by an attempt at rational thought modified by the limitation of individuals, institutions and scarce resources.

Clearly, the first and prime criterion is whether the project is academically sound. Sponsors usually look for evidence that the R & D workers are competent and that the project is well designed and looks capable of being effectively carried out. From the figures of SSRC it seems that a surprisingly high number of projects fail on this count, but assuming that there are still more projects than there are funds, other criteria are now applied. The second criterion is usually technical merit—does it contribute significantly to the discipline and to neighbouring disciplines? In a sense this is the same as relevance—the project must be relevant to major topics or a 'perceived need' within the discipline. Sponsors must rely heavily upon their expert and academic advisors in order to make such judgements. No doubt opinions vary and equally a consensus view is probably reached in most cases. A third criterion is sometimes asserted as social merit. In some senses it is possible to say that Project A contributes more to social welfare than Project B. This is probably only applicable for relatively extreme cases and one hesitates to give examples, although one finds it in the allocation problems between heart transplants and less glamorous fields within medical research, and certainly in the space/defence research controversies. There are fairly obvious problems in applying such crude criteria and in the end projects must somehow be approved or rejected on rather weak grounds.

In an attempt to improve the funding rationale, many sponsors are now busy preparing research policies which attempt to lay down guidelines for the sort of work which the sponsor feels should be supported and which thus helps to channel decisions along a more orderly path. By applying 'policy' criteria, as well as the normal criteria, it is no doubt hoped that a more rational basis for decision making could be achieved and that funds will be used more effectively. This raises quite serious points which are discussed more fully in Chapter 7.

At present it is clear that most Trusts have very loosely defined guidelines and have great freedom to make grants to any institution for any subject they think suitable. This freedom is a valuable asset and has been used effectively to support work which is of great use and yet which has for various reasons not found support from official bodies (see the interesting discussion by Dennis Hart, 1972). There is no denying, however, that the freedom allowed to sponsors within the allocation policy makes the applicant's task difficult and causes considerable variation in policy outcomes. It is a common place of researchers to find a project has been rejected by one body, but sponsored by another. While there may be ultimate grounds for satisfaction in finding support for the project somewhere, the time, effort and uncertainty involved in raising finance is both expensive and wasteful. There is a conflict here between efficiency in allocation which would both simplify the applicant's task and increase the pressures of accountability (either to Government Departments or to trustees), which formalize the grant awarding process, and the pluralism which (at some cost) allows researchers to approach several bodies. This cannot easily be resolved.

It has not been possible to identify the full extent of variation in policy outcomes. On the one hand policy guidelines are so loose it is not possible to relate allocation decisions to policy formulation, and on the other hand information about the projects supported is limited to the title and researcher, and it is therefore impossible to make judgements concerning the place of such projects in the light of past policy decisions by the sponsors. In other words, most sponsors allocate their funds over a wide range of projects and there seems to be no pattern of consistent support for one type of project rather than another. To some extent this mild confusion is compounded with the relative weights attached to education by sponsors. Obviously, almost all of the DES work is educational, all of Schools Council work is educational, but only about 20 per cent of SSRC money is spent on educational research, perhaps 20 per cent of Leverhulme, and about the same in the Nuffield Foundation. The extent of the involvement in educational research by sponsors varies significantly and when this is added to the variety of topics which seem to be supported, no pattern of allocation emerges.

One may now perhaps conclude with a few general remarks. Establishing criteria, or perhaps a research policy, is very different from making decisions about particular projects, and it is here that doubts and queries are raised as projects appear to meet the rather loose criteria and yet fail to gain support. By definition, the meetings of the various committees are confidential and no account of success or failure of particular projects need be given to applicants. Hence, it is impossible to establish the way in which decisions are made concerning research applications. It is no secret that personalities and their particular interests and prejudices play a significant part in such decisions and due weight needs to be given to the politics and sociology of the composition of advisory committees of the sponsors. Clearly, each application is considered by the advisory committee in the light of its technical merit; its relation to any perceived gaps in the relevant body of knowledge; and perhaps some estimate of its 'usefulness.' Thus, the claims of technical merit, academic merit, and social merit must be well considered by all committees. This still leaves room for judgements as to the relative value of the project and even the final decision must be balanced by such factors as the spread of grants between subjects and sectors; between institutions and perhaps between locations. Thus, no sponsor will allocate money continuously to a single university or for a particular project. This is quite understandable but the applicant now has problems. His project may be considered quite satisfactory, but a run of grants awarded to pre-school projects makes yet another study of early childhood not desirable; or perhaps two other projects have recently been funded at his university; or perhaps the subject area has already been fairly well covered and despite the quality of the project, 'something needs to be done elsewhere' and another project will gain preference for this reason. Although this leads to success for another applicant, the reasons for the rejection of some applicants is seldom disclosed and it seems to be very desirable that the policy be adopted of informing all rejected applicants of the reasons for the decisions. Any procedure which can increase the openness of decision making is desirable. At the very least researchers could expect to have, as with SSRC, the number of applicants and the rejection rate and, of course, a full explanation for all rejected applications. On the other hand, those in the position of having to give a full set of reasons for the rejection of applications might find this extremely burdensome and that a disproportionate amount of time and energy was being spent on a relatively fruitless task. One notes the point but the allocation of R & D funds is too important to be given less than the full attention it deserves.

CHAPTER 4

The Performers of Educational Research and Development

It is quite clear that the universities carry out most educational research. What is not so clear is whether the universities are capable of a large-scale sustained research effort. Casual evidence has long suggested that most educational research is concentrated in a few universities and that the production of postgraduate students is also associated with strong research interests. The phenomena of strong research activity with large numbers of postgraduate students is not a startling discovery: it is well established in the physical sciences and is in any case one of the main arguments in the justification for undertaking research work. Only with the involvement of postgraduate students in research work is the full benefit of R & D realized because the training benefits can be included with the prime benefits which are of course the knowledge and information obtained by the research work.

Tables 4.1 to 4.6 show how funds and projects are distributed between universities by subject area. The results reveal some interesting points.

The clearest point is the dominant position of London University. It is true that this is exaggerated due to the inclusion of all the Colleges and schools in the total funds for London University and as is well known, many of the largest Colleges are the same size as some other universities. Nevertheless, it is very interesting that London should take about a third of all resources and projects. It is a moot point whether this is 'desirable' or not in terms of research policy. On the one hand it seems to deny other universities the opportunity to expand their research work, but on the other hand London has built up staff, expertise and facilities to carry out work and it seems reasonable to take full advantage of the resources available. This is probably a non-problem in any case as the tables show a steady decline in the position of London as other universities build up research work, and one can expect this trend to develop.

The other very interesting point to be noted from the tables is that only about a dozen universities are able to mount a significant research effort. It is not possible to be precise about 'significant' but the tables record all universities with more than £30,000 in

TABLE 4.1: *Institutions which carry out educational R & D—I: The universities. Analysis by finance*

UNIVERSITY	1967/8		1968/9		1969/70		1970/1		1971/2	
	Finance	%	Finance	%	Finance	%	Finance	%	Finance	%
Birmingham	21,000	3·1	40,000	3·2	60,000	3·1	47,000	3·3	24,000	1·9
Bristol	21,000	3·1	50,000	4·0	52,000	3·4	50,000	3·5	46,000	3·6
Cambridge	37,000	5·4	54,000	4·4	72,000	4·7	69,000	4·8	68,000	5·3
Keele	11,000	1·6	34,000	2·7	54,000	3·5	51,000	3·5	35,000	2·8
Leeds	35,000	5·1	40,000	3·2	55,000	3·6	58,000	4·0	51,000	4·0
London	286,000	41·8	416,000	33·6	470,000	30·8	369,000	25·5	309,000	24·3
Manchester	62,000	9·1	85,000	6·9	84,000	5·5	62,000	4·3	28,000	2·2
Oxford	11,000	1·6	52,000	4·2	72,000	4·7	74,000	5·1	74,000	5·8
Wales	16,000	2·3	45,000	3·6	52,000	3·4	62,000	4·3	52,000	4·1
York	71,000	10·4	203,000	16·4	230,000	15·1	212,000	14·6	176,000	13·8
All Other	112,000	16·4	219,000	17·7	323,000	21·2	393,000	27·2	408,000	32·1
TOTAL	683,000	99·9	1,238,000	99·9	1,524,000	99·0	1,447,000	100·1	1,271,000	99·9

TABLE 4.2: *Institutions which carry out educational R & D—I: The universities. Analysis by projects*

UNIVERSITY	1967/8		1968/9		1969/70		1970/1		1971/2	
	Projects	%	Projects	%	Projects	%	Projects	%	Projects	%
Birmingham	8	5·8	14	6·9	16	6·4	13	5·3	8	4·7
Bristol	6	4·3	9	4·5	9	3·6	11	4·5	8	4·7
Cambridge	7	5·0	12	5·9	12	4·8	10	4·1	10	5·9
Keele	4	2·9	8	4·0	10	4·0	9	3·7	6	3·5
Leeds	5	3·6	6	3·0	11	4·4	10	4·1	7	4·1
London	37	26·6	48	23·8	67	24·4	56	23·0	41	24·0
Manchester	21	15·1	26	12·9	25	10·0	20	8·2	8	4·7
Oxford	4	2·9	6	3·0	8	3·2	8	3·3	7	4·1
Wales	7	5·0	9	4·5	11	4·4	10	4·1	7	4·1
York	4	2·9	9	4·5	11	4·4	14	5·6	12	7·0
All Other	36	25·9	55	27·2	76	30·4	82	33·7	57	33·3
TOTAL	139	100·0	202	100·2	250	100·0	243	99·6	171	100·0

TABLE 4.3: *Educational R & D in other institutions—resources 1967/8–1971/2*

INSTITUTION	1967/8		1968/9		1969/70		1970/1		1971/2	
	Resources	%	Resources	%	Resources	%	Resources	%	Resources	%
NCB	19,600		20,300		37,200		200		—	
NFER	201,600		236,700		223,700		288,000		295,000	
CVC and Principals	16,800		16,800		16,800		13,400		8,500	
Nuffield	24,000		55,000		55,000		48,200		54,000	
Other	59,200		115,000		149,500		146,300		80,470	
TOTAL	321,200		443,800		482,000		496,100		437,520	

TABLE 4.4: *Educational R & D in other institutions—projects 1967/8–1971/2*

INSTITUTION	1967/8		1968/9		1969/70		1970/1		1971/2	
	Projects	%	Projects	%	Projects	%	Projects	%	Projects	%
NCB	5		5		5		1		—	
NFER	14		18		16		24		20	
CVC and Principals	2		2		2		2		1	
Nuffield	2		2		2		2		2	
Other	20		39		53		41		19	
TOTAL	43		66		78		70		42	

1968/9 of externally funded research work. The fact that there are so few says something about the size of research funds available and also about the performance of research work in universities.

Those universities which do contribute substantially to educational research seem to fall into three groups. The first group are those who traditionally have always had a strong interest in education. It would be common knowledge in the profession that any list of contributors to educational research must include London, Bristol, Birmingham and Leeds and roughly in that order. It is here that most of the dominant figures in educational research have held their chairs and attract and encourage research workers to develop their ideas and techniques. It is also here that one finds greatest attention paid to postgraduate studies—and this point is developed later. There is no immediate explanation of why these universities should excel in educational research—how does one account for 'Centres of Excellence?'

The second group of universities are those which have strong political connections. Research funds are not always allocated in a way which allows of inspection and there are therefore no means of assessing how far funds may be influenced by strong personalities at the committee stage as well as by the quality of the research design and other criteria. There is nothing startling about this—indeed one could argue that patronage or commission would not be forthcoming at all unless such personal influences could be brought to bear. This pattern can be detected elsewhere: most of the Trusts and Foundations have academic advisors and it is not surprising to find projects funded at their universities, and many projects may originate within an organization itself. The actual placing and funding of the project is then subject to the usual pressures and decisions—except that the performer is often attached or related to the organization itself in some way. Again, there is nothing remarkable in these arrangements—so long as the criteria of academic, social, and economic merit can be met.

The third group of universities which contribute significantly to research work are those which one does not normally associate with educational research. It is possible that these are the universities which will expand and form a large part of research units around which further effort will be concentrated. To these must be added a fourth group not yet mentioned; the 'new' universities such as Brunel, Sussex and Lancaster, all of which have both political power and research expertise in education.

The work that is done is shown in Tables 4.5 and 4.6. It was hoped that such an analysis would indicate the existence of any specialisms or centres of excellence. In fact the tables show a rather

TABLE 4.5: *Distribution of funds by subject areas at universities 1968–1970*

	General	Economics, Finance, etc.	Architecture and Buildings	Admin. and Organization	Schools	Curriculum Studies	Psychology of Ed. (1)	Psychology of Ed. (2)	Sociology of Ed.	Academic Profession	Further Education	Higher Education	Counselling Service: VG	Educ. Ment. and Physic. Handicapped Children	TOTAL PROJECTS
Birmingham						26,000	11,800	48,300						13,500	99,600
Bristol					20,000	47,400			10,000	24,000					101,400
Cambridge	7,000	6,000	16,000			56,400	21,000	19,600							126,000
Keele	1,600					37,600	2,000	3,400		6,800	18,400	7,400	10,300		87,500
Leeds	1,300			7,400		57,300	5,700	500	3,700			8,300		8,400	92,600
London	1,300	74,400	40,700	12,600	350	551,100	13,400	51,800	76,400	11,500		44,500		6,700	884,750
Manchester	1,200			16,600	20,500	30,300	5,300	17,250	12,200	12,400	6,200	17,400		29,700	169,050
Oxford						12,800	9,500		89,200	1,800		500		10,200	124,000
Wales						22,700	4,000	70,200							96,900
York						398,000	6,300	20,900		7,100					432,300
All other Univ.	1,300	7,400	—	3,500	6,400	256,800	28,000	113,000	61,000	18,900	33,500	22,400	4,500	13,600	570,300
TOTAL	13,700	87,800	56,700	40,100	47,250	1,496,400	107,000	344,950	252,500	82,500	58,100	100,500	14,800	82,100	2,784,400

TABLE 4.6: *Distribution of projects by subject areas at universities 1968–1970*

	General	Economics, Finance, etc.	Architecture and Buildings	Admin. and Organization	Schools	Curriculum Studies	Psychology of Ed. (1)	Psychology of Ed. (2)	Sociology of Ed.	Academic Profession	Further Education	Higher Education	Counselling Service: VG	Educ. Ment. and Physic. Handicapped Children	TOTAL PROJECTS
Birmingham						8	5	12						5	30
Bristol					6	6			2	4					18
Cambridge	4	2	2			11	2	3							24
Keele	1					4	1	2		2	2	2	4		18
Leeds	1		1	1		5	2	1	2			2		2	17
London	1	9	6	3	1	35	5	21	15	3		6		4	109
Manchester	1			4	4	6	6	3	4	5	2	4		21	51
Oxford						2	6		2	1		1		2	14
Wales						9	3	8							20
York						12	4	2		2					20
All Other Universities	6	2	8	2	43	27	27	23	8	6	4	5	2	9	131
TOTAL	134	13	17	10	14	125	61	75	33	23	8	20	6	33	452

random allocation of subjects once the 'core' subject of curriculum studies and psychology are abstracted. Given the previous discussion of results in Chapter 2, this is not very surprising—these subjects account for well over 60 per cent of the total so that one would expect this to be distributed across most universities. The 'big' universities like London and Manchester then take most of the rest of the subject groups with a scatter of projects across the whole range of subjects. Other specialists are quickly noted—Keele's counselling and VG work, London's economic studies, and so on. No doubt as research work is developed other specialisms will be developed by other universities and attract workers in that area. The firm base for starting in educational research seems to be curriculum work and other studies then group around this central core.

The arguments for and against specialization need not be reported here (Robbins Report, para. 382 *et seq.*). Educational research is so much in its infancy that any good new project anywhere is to be welcomed. When education has the resources of, say, Chemistry or Biology then one can begin to issue warnings of duplication or of concentrating resources in certain departments for certain topics. At present the field is small enough for most workers to be familiar with the on-going research and the places and people doing the work. Unlike the physical sciences, there is little need for heavy investment in machines and equipment and hence 'specialists' move around and can often take their projects with them. The idea of the possibility of some subjects becoming specialist areas seems unlikely—although there are some exceptions already when one considers the science studies at Chelsea, London and Leeds, and language studies at York. Both these subjects require relatively more, and more specialist, equipment than other subject or curriculum studies and hence it is not too surprising to find some concentation of effort.

Much educational research is carried on outside Institutes and Departments of Education. It was hoped to demonstrate the volumes and nature of this activity but in many cases the data relating to the project revealed only the University, not the Department, and hence it is not possible to comment on this point. From the data sheets and from the London evidence alone one could guess that at least a third of the research is undertaken outside education departments. Elsewhere the figures might be even higher.

This balance of research effort is rather disturbing. It reflects what is one of the main points of this study—that educational research and the education of teachers and researchers should be more closely integrated. The interests of psycholinguists, sociologists and the growing interest of economists in education may not exhibit the same urgency in the improvement of educational performance as the training or practising teacher may wish: these interests are however quite fundamental to improvements in organization and teaching and learning performance. The fact exists that because some of the more basic or fundamental inquiries are undertaken outside education departments, and much of the applied research is located outside the universities the student of Education often fails to come to grips with research work aimed at *understanding* rather than *improving* learning and teaching.

Staff in education departments seem to divide their time in the same manner as those in the social sciences (see CVC survey 1972), and the earlier position described by W. Taylor's survey (in Young 1965) (which showed that pressure of time prevented much research) is now no longer an accurate picture of education departments in universities. Nevertheless, the *interests* of staff may be unchanged—and here Taylor's survey shows a pre-occupation with curricula work and similar research or with basic theory; above all an individualistic approach so common to Universities. There are, however, attempts to concentrate research work and advance study within schools or Units and in particular to link research with advanced postgraduate work.

The formation of Advanced Studies and Research Units located within Departments/Schools of Education seem to have developed quite rapidly in the last few years at London, Bristol and Manchester. Here there is a need to maintain a constant awareness of research, in order to satisfy the curiosity of advanced students, some of whom may become research workers themselves. At the same time the Advanced Studies Departments become a natural focus for research work and have the breadth and depth of resources to engage in serious work.

Work in other institutions

The nature and work of these institutions is fairly well known—one of the main virtues of a specialist institution is that it quickly becomes known for its work. There is no need to describe the NFER, NCB, Tavistock, NCET, or any of the other institutions noted in Appendix I.

The work carried out at such institutions is usually more applied or action orientated than research at universities. Partly this derives from deliberate policy: there is a determination to apply research methods to practical or 'real' problems and partly it derives from the fact that much (perhaps half) of all research work is externally financed. This almost certainly implies that the sponsor requires a policy-orientated or applied research report and the research efforts therefore are directed towards practical problems. Examples can be readily drawn from the programmes of any of the independent institutions—the Educational Arrangements for Immigrant Pupils project at NFER; the study of Adopted and Illegitimate children at NCB bear interest to the applied work undertaken at these organizations.

None of these institutions either trains research workers or has particularly close and continuing relations with teachers. It is true that the NFER has many contacts with schools and teachers in the course of its research programmes, but there is no lasting contact such as that given in short courses, in-service training, etc. So far as one can see, very few of the other institutions operate courses either, although it is known that Tavistock offer short courses in psychology. In some cases the terms of the trust deed or the policy documents which form the basis of the institution prevent such activities, but in other cases it is simply 'not policy' to do so.

One is then faced with a curious situation. The teachers and advanced students of Education who should have a close interest in applied or policy-orientated work are trained and taught in universities which tend to have either basic and fundamental research interests, or a concern with curricula and other development work. Perhaps this is one of the causes of the present discontent between researchers and teachers. It is a minor but interesting point that if closer integration of research institutions and the results of applied research and the schools and colleges could be facilitated, some of this discontent might be erased—but the difficulties of implementing this are formidable. It is possible to query the raison d'être of independent research institutions: they are after all only performing work which *could* be carried out in Universities and they are usually more expensive agencies of R & D for that very reason, i.e. they have overheads to carry which are not financed by UGC funds.

There are two broad answers to the point: (1) that activities other than R & D are an important part of the institutes' activities (as with the institute of Race Relations), and (2) that full-time, large-scale permanent involvement is the most effective means of organizing R & D. Both arguments are sound and the matter is argued at some length in the next chapter.

Research and researchers

It has frequently been remarked that the growth of educational research is constrained as much by the shortage of researchers as by the availability of funds. Wiseman (1962) remarked that an increase in research funds would be an embarrassment and 'This is because of the shortage of man and machines—and the organization to employ these effectively' (see also Taylor, 1971; Pidgeon, 1971). The position has not altered much since then and has been a recurring theme not only in this country but elsewhere (Edwards, 1968; Yates, 1971). What is badly needed is some data on the output of MA, MSc and MEd students. It is not possible to detect them directly because most Universities do not offer an MEd and do not distinguish the MA/MSc by subject in their lists of higher degrees awarded. The same comment, of course, applies to doctorates.

Two points need to be clearly stated. Firstly, there is only a loose relation between higher degrees obtained and the number of researchers available, and secondly, not all higher degrees are a good preparation for educational research. There is a third point to be made: in planning terms the estimated number of educational researchers 'needed' and the number actually *demanded*, i.e. who can be employed through research grants, etc., is very uncertain and is something on which the SSRC and HERU are currently engaged.

That many students who receive higher degrees do not continue to do research is an assertion based on the most casual of evidence. There is a strong suspicion that many students take higher degrees as a means of gaining promotion within teaching and educational administration rather than a preparation for educational research. There is no evidence for this as no studies exist of postgraduate students' occupational choice and subsequent career. Any expansion of postgraduate training in educational research must consider this point carefully.

The related point is of course that at present many MA/MEd courses are primarily advanced studies/courses and are not closely related to research techniques. It is difficult to generalize because the image of subjects and options included in postgraduate Education degrees is so varied: but one can be fairly sure that it is not obvious that sound training in educational research can be obtained on a 'traditional' Master's course. The need still exists for courses which offer a good training in R & D techniques while also providing an advanced course in the particular subject area with educational research. It is not easy to balance the two requirements but a number of universities have recently reviewed their postgraduate studies programme and established new courses which attempt to do this, and the SSRC review of their postgraduate training awards is likely to encourage some re-thinking of course requirements.

In any reappraisal of postgraduate courses it should be noted that the universities which produce the largest number of postgraduate research students are those which do most research. This confirms the picture of the physical sciences and demonstrates the need for a sound research and postgraduate flow with which to build up more research (Massey Report, Great Britain, Council for Scientific

Policy, 1971). This good research work attracts research students and the students often transfer or progress from advanced courses, or are attracted into Education Departments by interesting on-going work.

There are, of course, some problems. On the one hand, all research workers need to be reminded that the ultimate success of educational research must be seen in the improved performance of schools, administrators, teachers, and pupils. The time-span of research, invention, innovation and utilization—the diffusion of invention—is of course critical and often unknown, although the justification of research is independent of time. On the other hand, it is often the case that educational research, particularly outside Education Departments—but sometimes within them—is not closely identified with teachers, schools and pupils. Education is simply a convenient area in which to pursue some sociological or psychological work, and the schools are good laboratories which, like hospitals, yield 'clinical material'. The danger of this is fairly clear: that the researchers, unfamiliar with the educational system, will be confused by the complexity of the system and their work will lose something of value. A balanced view would be that much fundamental and applied research should be carried out within education departments and that closer links between psychology, sociology, economics and other departments with an interest in education can be established. This should ensure that research workers outside Education gain something of the 'feel' of educational practice and institutions.

It is mainly for this reason that many regard teaching experience as an essential requirement of any researcher. This is another recurring theme of many conferences and papers that has good points arranged on both sides and no definitive conclusion. For many types of school based research it is very valuable to have teaching experience. For some kinds of basic research it is not at all necessary. Perhaps the most important point is the time scale and personal factors involved if researchers are to have teaching experience. By the time a potential researcher has graduated, has acquired some teaching experience and some facility with basic research techniques he or she is in the mid-late 20s and is probably facing marriage, family, and/or mortgage. It is not likely that many can, or will, enter the insecurity of research work at that time and even if they were willing the salary required is often not forthcoming. It suggests therefore that most research is carried out by younger staff direct from University or College—and indeed many do fall into this category and thus have no teaching experience. Guided by more experienced staff it is unlikely that lack of teaching practice is a serious impediment to many kinds of educational research.

Finally, one must mention the fact that educational researchers have no career pattern. It is usually assumed that research is associated with teaching in universities and colleges: hence the career of a researcher is related to the higher education system. It is now gradually being accepted that some, if not most, educational research is best carried out full-time (whether in teams with full statistical and computing facilities or with perceptive observation and experimental work in schools). In both cases full clerical assistance and other minimum research backing is necessary. Teaching and research cannot always be combined satisfactorily and the researcher becomes dependent on the permanency of a teaching system peripheral or external to his main interests and work.

This is partially recognized by the establishment of research fellows and the system of research officers and professors whose teaching duties are nominal or zero but whose salary is linked to the normal teaching scale. The difficulty of course is that these appointments are usually contractual and the tendency is thus for research work to be carried out by young staff who then seek the security of permanent teaching positions and carry on research in their available non-teaching time. This limits both research and staff but is the way in which most educational research—indeed most social science work—is carried out in this country.

To return to the main point of this section: educational research workers are unknown in quality or quantity, either present or future. We know not how many we require nor where they may come from, nor how or where they should be trained in the different research techniques. There is the sharp distinction between workers completing higher degrees and workers remaining in research—but the spillover of well trained individuals into administrative positions must carry interesting implications of its own. Finally, there is the not so long-term problem of careers for research workers which remains unconsidered.

All in all, the relation between educational research and the supply of researchers remains unresolved and is in urgent need of careful investigation by SSRC and DES.

CHAPTER 5

The Organization of Educational Research and Development

Introduction

The wide range and complexity of the topics which impinge on any discussion of the organization of educational research is remarkable and makes any division of the material extremely difficult. There are some untidy relations between the definitions of R & D discussed earlier in the context of basic research versus development and the objectives of R & D discussed now in the context of organizational arrangements. Similarly, the discussion of innovation and utilization in Chapter 7 could be related to earlier work, but, given the complexity of the subject, a neat, logical sequential approach is most difficult to attain.

First, it is necessary to make clear the objectives of educational R & D and to note both the different priorities attached to them and the way in which these priorities influence the institutional arrangements. There is then the need to consider the market for R & D, particularly the production relations for the production and transmission of knowledge and information, and the institutions which comprise the market. Traditionally, the market has been quite sharply divided among those who produce knowledge, those who sponsor learning and/or commission information, and those who use it. Transmission mechanisms have been neglected and there is a need for such interests to operate in the market. The complex relations between sponsors, performers, and users are changing and the situation requires examination.

The problems associated with R & D outputs—the use of knowledge and information to improve educational practice, and aid decision making—also needs discussion, particularly as the criterion supporting research is increasingly associated with relevance and value in use. Allocation criteria must certainly be considered. The relations between the production and use of information are complex and various models of the research—invention—development—innovation—adoption cycle have been proposed or assumed. Such a model is useful in explaining the time span between production and use of information and is necessary for any understanding of innovation in education. Finally, there must be some account of international experience. Much of the theoretical and empirical work in R & D organization derives from the US but some European countries—notably Sweden—have devoted a great deal of thought and resources to these problems.

It is not easy to separate these topics for rational discussion but some selection and arrangement is necessary. The discussion of the market relations for educational R & D is placed in this chapter, an account of international experience follows in Chapter 6, while the problems associated with decision criteria, and the production and utilization of research outputs form the concluding Chapter, 7.

The objectives of educational R & D.

There seems to be no clear statement anywhere in the literature of the objectives of educational R & D, although one can, of course, find a number of statements which approximate to such objectives. The objectives of R & D are different from the *definitions* of R & D given in Chapter 2, but it is interesting to relate them. The objectives then can be stated as:

'Research has come to be applied to such a wide range of activities within the field of education that it has ceased to have a single identifiable meaning' (Travers, 1964, p. 4). His definitions include . . . 'A scientific body of knowledge about education should enable the educator to determine just what teaching and other learning conditions to provide in order to produce desired aspects of learning behaviour among young people who attend school' (p. 5).

Alternatively . . . 'educational research is concerned with producing information which is needed to make improvements in education' . . . and again 'It is information . . . which must ultimately be useful to those who have the responsibility for decision making in education' (Hayman Jr., 1968).

Again . . . 'Conference . . . confirms the view that a rapid expansion of research into the many facets of education is essential to help in making decisions into such matters as organization, processes and curriculum' (Radford, 1967).

Or again, 'Those who sponsored the conference and those who participate in it . . . are, for the most part, committed to the proposition that its justification in the short or long term must rest on the contribution it can make to the improvement of educational practice' (Yates, 1971).

And finally, 'Educational Research is now accepted as a necessary element in the multifarious educational activities of any sophisticated society . . . By its work it is expected that policies, structures, methods and curricula will be improved and refined so that the educational process and the educational system will become more efficient and more effective' (Wiseman, intro. to Cane & Schroeder, 1971, p. vii).

In short, one can argue that educational research should:

(1) advance the body of knowledge of those disciplines which form the subject matter of education;

(2) contribute a stream of information to the educational decision-makers;

(3) improve the teaching/learning process and other practices within the educational system.

It is now possible to turn to the institutional arrangements for the production of knowledge and information (which is taken to be the prime task of R & D) and the fulfilment of the other objectives of R & D.

The organization of educational research in this country is deceptively simple. On the one hand, there are the relatively few sponsors—DES, Schools Council, Nuffield and SSRC, *et al.*—and on the other hand, there is a large array of performers—NFER, the half dozen or so Universities which carry out a substantial volume of research and all the remaining Universities together with a few specialist bodies such as NCB, Tavistock Institute of Human Relations, the Institute of Community Studies, etc.

A short examination reveals that the system is really quite complex. Sponsors—particularly SSRC and Nuffield but also DES and Schools Council—do some research work themselves; and performers—notably the Universities and NFER—devote some of their own resources to research. It is also the case that some bodies such as NCET which are not primarily R & D orientated do commission some work and also perform some work themselves. Again, the users—teachers, administrators, and the neglected elements such as parents, citizens, etc.—are represented in varying strengths on the various governing bodies and committees of the sponsors and performers and have some influence on what projects shall be performed and financed. It is also the case (Chapter 3) that sponsors vary in their criteria for selection of projects, and again (Chapter 4) that the type of work performed varies a little between performers.

The relationships between these bodies are characterized by the diffuse, haphazard and unsystematic formal relations and the equally loose but relatively close and complete network of informal communications based on personal contacts. Such arrangements are possible because of the small size of the R & D market but the efficiency and desirability of such arrangements are open to question. There are certainly no clear lines of communication or machinery for consultation, advice and control; and there does not appear to be a central body which is capable of creating a strategy for educational research, or relating R & D to innovation, utilization and evaluation. Sponsors and performers are thus separated both by function and by institutional arrangements and there is no body which allows formal consultations on matters of common interest. Some recent attempts have however been made under the chairmanship of Professor W. Taylor and it is to be hoped that these will continue.

The market must, of course, include a third interest group—the users. These represent a diverse group comprising teachers, administrators at local and national level, academics and researchers and of course the children, parents and other social groups who have an interest in the understanding and improvements of the educational system. The significance of the users will be discussed at length later: attention is first directed to the performer-sponsor relationship.

A model of the market for educational R & D

The traditional model is that sponsors remain passive and sift through the applications for grants with the help of a panel of experts. Those who manage to obtain grants are then fairly free to pursue their own work. It is true that most sponsors require some account of the work undertaken with the help of their funds but, subject to the preparation of a report to sponsors, there are few constraints on the talents and interests of the researcher. The onus of 'demand' is left to individuals working in Universities and the independent institutions. This represents a practice well in the tradition of the Arts and Humanities scholarship, where individuals pursue their own interests seeking financial support from external sources as and when they feel it necessary.

The accountability or control exercised by sponsors varies both in method and intensity. Some sponsors have virtually no control—the applicant is given full responsibility for the use of the funds although naturally any resulting publication will carry acknowledgement of the supporting body and expectation of such publication will be a factor in the award of a grant. Most of the large sponsors however exercise some system of control. The Schools Council and NCET have a monitoring system whereby field officers or senior staff regularly visit projects and report progress. The SSRC require an annual report on progress and the DES usually ask for regular interim reports as well as the terminal report. These controls are not onerous and although they are clearly designed to establish some guidelines for the researchers engaged on the project, they do not usually act as severe constraints on the 'freedom' of the researcher (see discussion by Chase 1968, 1969).

The traditional model has many advantages. It allows freedom to individuals to seek funds when and from whom they wish; it permits a variety of alternative sources to which they can apply for educational and non-educational topics, and it allows sponsors to be flexible in the allocation of funds—which is something much prized by sponsors. The researcher is free to follow his talents and, subject to the period of the grant and a terminal report, is not tied to excessive external pressures. Those sponsors who seek to commission work—who deliberately act as 'customers' have been able to secure contractors to do the work because the market was still small enough for sponsors to be informed of current on-going work and the interests and expertise of various researchers. In most cases the 'active' sponsors who commissioned work were DES or NCET and suitable devices were developed to enable the customer to monitor the progress of the contractor. However, it is argued shortly that the market structure is gradually changing, primarily because the more 'active' or 'directive' activities of sponsors have not been matched by a response from the traditional 'demand' side of the market.

The loosely knit organization of educational research is small enough to avoid duplication and yet large enough to offer the advantages of some specialization. Thus, there are sponsors con-concerned with schools and the curriculum; with educational technology; with the universities and higher education; and many of the private Foundations will sponsor work into 'general problems'. The problems of basic research in psychology and sociology are associated with the universities and, of course, the NFER operates on a wide range of problems. In short, the existing organizations do not seem to be lacking in variety and breadth of interests amongst sponsors—and hence presumably among the performers.

Much of the success of this pattern of organization depends on the related linear model of R & D results. Here is it often assumed that R & D leads to invention—theories, practices, materials, etc. which in turn will be developed into innovations which are then adopted by the users through the usual channels of dissemination. If this linear model operates successfully, then clearly the roles of sponsor, performer and user can remain separate, being linked merely by a loose network of communications which permits some diffusion of results after a suitable development period. Given the diffuse nature of 'the user' and an even 'looser' network of dissemination, there is something to be said for the present pattern of the R & D market where work is carried out by performers who are largely divorced from both sponsor and user. It ensures that the research is performed well because the worker is personally involved in it and is being creative, undisturbed by external pressures of policy, teaching or other 'user requirements'. The fact that the work is sponsored implies that at least some criterion of 'usefulness' has been satisfied and perhaps this is sufficient rationale for enabling the market to remain undisturbed. Rothschild, of course, could not accept this and if most sponsored R & D work is based on customer-contractor principles then the market structure will be significantly altered.

Changes in the traditional passive model

It can also be noted that some sponsors seem to be by-passing performers and establishing research units of their own, as with SSRC and Schools Council. The sponsor-performer relationship is, in these cases, being short-circuited into a collapsed single system where the sponsor is also the performer and in a few cases the user.

It is clear from several documents and reports that the present model is unsatisfactory in a number of ways—most notably in that selection of project areas should not be left to the vagaries of the market or the fashion conscious researchers or sponsor. It is often claimed that user requirements are ignored in the programme offered by performers, that researchers are tackling problems and areas unrelated to the 'real' problems of the educational system. Much then depends on who the user is likely to be. A moment's thought reveals a wide assortment of 'requirements' and it is not surprising that some feel that the bulk of educational research is irrelevant to their needs. The needs of DES, teachers, and academic researchers are more likely to be competitive than complementary. Cane & Schroeder (1971), for example, chronicle the nature of the teachers' dissatisfaction with research work, and the discontent among many administrators is admirably expressed by Orlans (1968). (See also Thatcher, 1970; Taylor, 1972; and Wiseman, 1973; SSRC Annual Reports, 1969/70 and 1970/1; and for a more general debate Rothschild & Dainton Reports, 1971).

Another view is that large areas of the field remain untouched—that gaps need to be filled in, say, pre-school education or that we know little about the learning abilities and achievements of undergraduates. The implication is that 'someone' should do some work in this area and this immediately reveals the weakness of the present passive model of the R & D market. This weakness is further exposed by another comment which has been made: that research now often needs to be large scale, sophisticated, 'bureau' based and long term. Only by following samples over several years can useful work be carried out in some areas and hence the individual performer, however creative, is unlikely to have the ability—in the sense of resources available—to successfully carry out the work (see SSRC Annual Reports 1969/70; 1970/1).

It is not too surprising, then, to find that in the last few years the pattern of the R & D market has been changing. Sponsors have been reviewing their criteria and seeking a change in performers. More attention has been paid to the needs of users (particularly if they are the sponsors) and, while no guides or machinery for improving the dissemination of results or the relation between research dissemination and innovation exist, at least the beginnings of concern for utilization of results are apparent (SSRC Conference papers 1971). The factors affecting the changed market conditions can now be examined.

The nature and location of educational R & D

The first area of change is the nature of educational research work and the location of such work. If research is to take the form of large scale statistical exercises using large samples of cross section/longitudinal data then permanent, full-time, research staff are needed. If detailed case studies based on close observation and sensitive interviewing are thought more appropriate then long-term work is usually involved and this too requires permanent staff and the necessary supporting services. It is surprising that we have so little knowledge of the best working environment.

Lazarfeld and Sieber (1964) claimed that in the USA 'most research on human behaviour is no longer produced by individual scholars': that most work was performed by Bureau research—a genetic term covering all Units, Centres, Institutes, etc. independent of, although perhaps attached to, Universities. It is also generally known that scientific and technological work has been organized like this for decades partly owing to the cost of the material and equipment, but equally through the need to sustain research teams over quite long periods of time to cope with the data and analysis problems associated with the research programme.

Lazarfeld and Sieber surveyed in 1962 all schools of education (63) or Deans of the graduate faculties in the 94 universities which had in the 1967/8 session granted at least 10 PhDs. All institutions made returns and the results showed that 39 of the universities engaged in educational research and some 108 units, departments, centres, etc. were identified. Thirty-six of these were subsequently eliminated because they were not research institutes but field testing services, demonstration or training units. The final sample consisted of 60 research institutes established in 36 universities. Although the survey is now 10 years old the authors' questions and conclusions are still relevant to the present discussion. (1) They note that most of the large-scale projects are now conducted in research institutes or bureaux, but that much educational research is still pursued by individuals. (2) They comment on the ambiguous role of research in the schools of education and the difficulties endemic in the teaching, training and supervisory work undertaken by education departments. (3) They draw attention to the service elements in educational research. (4) They note that much educational research is performed by quasi independent institutes concerned with testing and evaluation—the Psychological Corporation and the Educational Testing Service, which have no parallel in the social sciences. (5) Finally, they note that because there is no strong reference group among educational researchers, there is great difficulty in utilizing and disseminating results to teachers, clients and other practitioners. 'Failure in application makes the role of client demand a critical factor in the arrangement of research and in the opportunities for feed-back from the practical situation' (Lazarfeld and Sieber 1964).

They develop each of these ponts and then focus on the key problems in educational research: service *v* research; careers for educational researchers; the 'climate of research in schools of education'; and the problems of dissemination and feed-back. These four problems have been recurring elements of much discussion of the educational scene in this country and the work of Michael Young (1965) and W. D. Wall (1962) and others will be discussed. It is interesting to reflect that this American work completed nearly a decade ago is still the main source of knowledge we have of social science research practice.

Attitudes to educational R & D

Teachers, administrators and others concerned with the educational scene are skilled, intelligent and articulate. They are usually deeply attached to their work and ask for little more than the opportunity to tackle their work without distraction. They constantly seek to improve their performance, to change and update methods, curricula and organization in order to meet their own high expectations. Hence, they seek information relating to improvement of operations, and educational research is therefore geared to '*their improvement* rather than the *understanding* of education' (Lazarfeld and Sieber, 1964).

What is demanded are aids to teachers and administration in the performance of their tasks and the improvement of their skills. This fact is demonstrated by the founding of most of the US research institutes—at Illinois, 1918, Ohio State and many other early established centres where the prime task was testing, 'problem surveys', and other services to area schools. This concept of educational research is still held strongly in this country. The image of the NFER was for a long period associated with test construction and similar services to LEAs, and the Guidance & Assessment Service is still a large and important unit of the Foundation. Opinions among clients may not be changing at all—Cane and Schroeder's useful study (1970) shows clearly that teachers select topics which are of direct application to their work—i.e. seeking improvement in skills and operations rather than an intellectual understanding of educational change and processes. Thus, teachers and training; streaming and the organization of groups for effective teaching; curriculum development and examination and assessment dominate the list of research requirements by teachers in the sample. This evidence simply confirms the earlier work of Taylor (1965).

It is perhaps surprising to find that educational researchers share these attitudes. Lazarfeld and Sieber tested the research institutes on a 10-point scale from Applied to Basic research. Researchers were asked to indicate: (1) their preferred position, and (2) their actual position on the scale. Exactly the same questions were given to a sample of social science research institutes. Education institutes revealed a mean position of 4·7 and social researchers 6·6, but what is most significant is that the *preferred* position of education (5·7) is still closer to applied research than the perceived actual position of social science researchers (6·6). A similar picture is obtained from Young and Taylor's small survey of Universities in 1965. When asked which topics deserved most attention, teaching methods, curriculum, school structure and organization, and specialist subject studies dominate the replies. (It is interesting to relate this to the teacher opinions in Cane and Schroeder, 1971).

Service and R & D

One can see from the above that the service element in educational research is still a powerful factor affecting the nature of the research undertaken and the organization of the research market. While one can applaud the apparent unity of purposes of researchers and teachers in both expectations and performance of educational research, there are some dangers.

The major point to be made here is that a preponderance of service work discourages research workers. This has happened in the US according to Lazarfeld and Siever (1964, pp 34–41) and has been noted by others. At present there is relatively little work of this kind available in the UK and hence the danger is small. Nevertheless, the foundations for a rapid expansion of service activities have been and are being, laid and in the next decade pressure on research staff will be severe. One thinks, for example, of such activities (which are research orientated or research based) as counselling, vocational and educational guidance, curriculum evaluation, attitude tests, measures of achievement and ability tests. Most of these services are at present in the research or in the development stage but there are already courses for counselling and guidance and regular courses designed to prepare teachers and others to administer and score tests. Once a research project reaches this stage then researchers are no longer needed, although staff trained and experienced in research techniques may be required.

This highlights the problem. Service work tends to discourage the recruitment of research staff. The two tasks demand rather different skills and interests and it is found that good research staff become restless if the service type work takes up a large part of their time. The evidence for such assertions is both scattered and casual. One finds it in the studies of industrial R & D establishments (Allison [Ed.], 1969) and in the larger consultancies (Raisbeck, 1965) and finally there is the well known phenomenon that research staff in Universities are more contented and perhaps more productive when removed from the routine activities of administration, students, and examinations duties. There is some formal recognition of this in the appointment of full-time research staff, although one can certainly find support for the view that teaching and research are complementary as much as competitive activities. It is also suggested as one of a number of reasons for the slow development of the Educational R & D centres in the US. Only when the preponderance of their work lay in the research end of the research/development/dissemination spectrum have they become 'acceptable' to the universities from which they recruit most of their staff. At the same time it means that the dissemination of best practices to schools was inadequately performed: and this is one of the prime reasons for the introduction of the RELs (Chase, 1970; Boyan, 1969; Mason and Boyan, 1968).

The pressure, however, will grow on University Departments and Institutes and on independent research organizations to conduct service work and to aid in the evaluation of curriculum change and other development work. Schools and LEAs will most probably seek to extend the range of their advisory services and the dissemination of information and adoption of new innovations will probably form a significant part of this work. Similarly, the Schools Council's drive towards dissemination of best practice will further draw on the scarce resources of qualified research manpower. One does not wish to over-emphasize the problem: such pressures lie in the immediate future but the relationship between service work and research is a delicate one and there is every reason to treat the US experience seriously and to anticipate the problems before they become too serious.

The location of R & D

The importance of research within bureaux or institutes compared with the traditional university department contribution can now be discussed. They have certain obvious advantages in the promotion of valuable, large-scale research work. First, they operate full-time on research unhindered by teaching, supervisory or other duties. Second, they offer the advantages of size and specialization: a library service, statistical services, and clerical and administrative facilities essential to large-scale research effort. The third advantage is the ability to train research staff at least as effectively as university departments and perhaps more effectively in terms of research techniques and the organization of research projects. There are usually regular project services; access to specialist consultants in related areas; and the stimulating atmosphere of a research-orientated centre. This helps to explain both the value and popularity of such independent Institutes as NFER, Tavistock, Institute of Community Studies, and the Advance Studies Centres and research units and institutes attached to universities. Not least they have the size and specialisms to be able to deal satisfactorily with service and research elements. Given a range of activities, it should be possible to relate personnel and work load in a more effective fashion than can a university. Judged by the growth of these separate units the advantages of separating research from teaching and service work seem to have been recognized by sponsors, particularly by the Research Councils which have invested heavily in this form of organization. Indeed, one could argue that the success and growth have been too successful—that the first doubts of divorcing units from teaching and administrative influences are perhaps beginning to be heard—that internal communications are poor; that senior staff in units do not or cannot operate effectively in both university departments and units; that research activity does not have external benefits which accrue to the university.

To summarize this first discussion, therefore—the organization of educational research is at present still based on the pattern of a few major sponsors; a large number of performers; individually operated projects; tackling work which is often service orientated/influenced; and constrained by teaching and supervisory duties. Changes are slowly taking place which call for independent or quasi-independent bureaux or Advanced Study Centres which will operate on full-time, large scale projects well supported by ancillary staff. These units may, or may not, be located at universities. This trend must surely be encouraged.

Changes in sponsors' requirements

The second factor affecting the organization of educational research is the growing awareness amongst sponsors that some review of the various fields is necessary so that the criteria of 'valuable' can be judged in relation to the existing volume and quality of the work in that area. If work in certain fields is to be carried out, who are the performers? The passive model sketched earlier indicates that the sponsor should wait until someone is willing to work in the field —which implies both the resources and ability to operate successfully in the field of interest to the sponsor.

Many sponsors are unwilling to wait. They actively seek investigators who will work on the particular problem or area. This is a familiar pattern in the natural and medical sciences, but is somewhat new in the social sciences with the major exception of the government departments who do commission research work of interest to the department. Examples are the hospital service, housing and social services, and of course DES. In recent years this sponsorship has become specifically tied to policy problems within departments and hence the scope of the work commissioned for the central government has diminished. Other sponsors may now consider taking active steps to pursue their lines of interest. The preliminary steps towards this is usually a policy review which, as was seen in the last chapter, is now pre-occupying a larger number of the Trusts. A 'natural' or understandable outcome of this exercise is the desire by the sponsor to adopt a more directive role than the traditional model allows.

It is at this point that doubts are cast on the efficiency with which the contemporary research market operates. The traditional passive model sketched earlier would predict that when sponsors have made their overviews of the research scene and established priorities they should await the arrival of proposals and applications which meet the established criteria. Actually, in a 'purely' passive model sponsors would have no need to make policy directing overviews. Providing gross imbalance within the allocation procedure were avoided, technical merit and the 'first come, first served' principles of allocation would be sufficient. However, granted that overviews are made and objectives and priorities are established, how do sponsors transact their requirements/policies to the market?

Market signals

Information is usually the first step—journals, newsletters, conferences and the research/development grapevine. If this fails to secure suitable proposals, then the sponsor may seek research more actively by direct requests to suitable people. Finally, if this still does not produce proposals the sponsor may engage research staff directly and conduct its own research work, on the topics pre-selected as areas of highest priority. Examples of these recent developments are not too difficult to find. The DES, of course, operates like this, as do the Home Office, DHSS, and other Government departments. The SSRC research units in industrial relations and race relations are employed directly by SSRC although they operate within university departments. The Schools Council research units—on examinations—are based at Great Portland Street, and the NCET also funds research work directly both at universities (Sussex) and within the organization at Great Portland Street. Such activity is likely to be increased rather than diminished and some changes to the model must be noted.

The DES has certainly adopted what seems to be a firm policy which was well presented by Mrs Thatcher as discussed earlier. This policy implies 'the active procurement of work by the Department on problems of its own choosing within a procedure and timetable which were relevant to its needs' (Thatcher, 1970). Another change—more gradual but probably more important—has been apparent in the work of the SSRC. It has become common practice for the subject boards to make overviews of their fields in order to place the individual projects within the framework of available knowledge, and projects are more likely to be supported if their topics fall into relatively unexplored areas of the subject. The demands of confidentiality and access to internal data for purposes of policy formulation also make change almost inevitable. The change in DES research policy is an obvious example. The SSRC is committed primarily to advances in knowledge but it is noticeable that the recently adopted active or directive role requires information on which to develop a strategy or policy for research. Information is available only through research/inquiry and hence funds are diverted to such purposes: the manpower forecasting in the social sciences, the subject overviews and the identification of gaps in knowledge. In the same way, and for more practical reasons, the CVC have both performed and commissioned research to aid policy making on selection for higher education and in a rather similar spirit NCET does some research, as does the Schools Council.

It may well be that such work would be justified on any criteria: but it so happens that the selection and performance of the work was made by the users concerned. It reveals a weakness in the market arrangements for the production of knowledge that could have interesting and perhaps serious implications. If there is no mechanism for the claims of all users to be heard it is likely that the sponsors will increasingly support work which has an air of relevance, particularly if the sponsor is likely to be an interested user of the results. The greater the degree of 'policy' formulation undertaken by sponsors, the more they need information and hence the more likely it is that they become significant users of the research they sponsor.

The pattern, then, is increasingly for the sponsor to begin to define objectives and, if performers are not coming forward to work, then the sponsor recruits its own staff directly. Such a policy has obvious implications: the effect on the career pattern of research workers; the nature and subject of research; the effect on existing research institutions and not least on the resources available for the remaining performers. These points are taken up in the next chapter.

The scale of resources available

The third factor affecting the organization of educational research is the scale and composition of resources. At present the scale of provision is probably too small, although the difficulties of establishing any normative or empirical criteria for allocations has been discussed. The composition of resources, however, is closely related to government allocations. Directly, the State contributes about 25 per cent and, if the government funds voted to the SSRC and Schools Council are included, the central and local government contribute over 70 per cent of our research resources. There is nothing surprising in this—it is usually the case (see Yates, 1971). There are, however, certain facets of this relationship which need some comment. There is first the view, discussed by Yates, that if most government research funds were channelled through the universities there would be a bias toward basic research. This is possible but unlikely in the current situation—any project which is secured by a university department is likely to have competed with other projects from a variety of other departments and institutions. If it is basic research, it is because the sponsor approved of the work, and not because the university insisted on basic work.

The danger, of course, is the reverse of this position: that because, directly and indirectly, government departments influence the volume of resources available, there is the demand for a return of some kind on research activity. That return is increasingly taking the form of policy-orientated studies and the demand for information relevant to planning, administration, and other uses, notably, of course, for the practitioners—the teachers and administrators. In this climate the allocation criterion is relevance to the user/sponsor and the flow of funds to basic research is likely to be reduced. In short, the scarce resources available to the market encourage sponsors to adopt rather hard allocation criteria and this perhaps tends to reduce the availability of funds for basic work.

The market would be influenced substantially as much by an abundance of resources as by the present scarcity. There is every reason to suppose that the delicate balance of interests between sponsors, performers and users would be put under severe strain. On one hand there is already concern at the duplication of interests, projects, and competitive rather than complementary work on-going at universities and research establishments. If the scale of resources increases, so the pressure to generate more projects and expand existing ones also increases. The probability of duplication is now magnified and sponsors (and users) would dislike this. Some work, of course, can usefully be duplicated but as far as possible work should be complementary rather than competitive and there is a need for some mechanism which permits, and indeed encourages, a proper flow of information.

On the other hand, performers are likely to be concerned about the delays in decision making by sponsors if increased numbers of applications extend still further what is already a lengthy process of negotiation and decision making before grants and contracts are awarded (or rejected). There is something frustrating to performers in the problem of joint application to sponsors: it is obviously quicker and safer to the performer to tender grant applications to more than one sponsor, but naturally sponsors dislike such activities and the whole process of obtaining sponsored funds becomes a very delicate operation. If resources for educational research increase it is possible that the passive model of the R & D market would give way to a more closely coordinated clearing house system which would tend to adopt a directive rather than passive role. Such a tendency is perhaps a natural consequence of a more centralized system but it is quite probable that a deliberate attempt at policy formulation would be made. The precedents of the Research Councils, the Trusts and Foundations all suggest such an approach: as funds become centrally allocated so a rationale for allocation is needed and this can seem to lead naturally into 'a policy for research'. The signs are at present weak and would no doubt be resisted by many, but 'accountability' can be a powerful inducement to more directive policies. Once more one must contrast pluralism in funding with the efficiency and accountability of allocation. The implications of this possibility are discussed in Chapter 7.

Conclusion

The traditional passive model of the R & D market is under pressure from at least three factors and changes have been taking, and are likely to take place. There is a dissatisfaction with the output of the current market and the view that 'better' results could be obtained from specialist units, centres or other independent research establishments where teams can be housed to do full time research work unhampered by other duties. There is also some kind of research policy. Policy reviews are made—perhaps as part of allocation criteria—and once priorities are established, there is a tendency for sponsors actively to direct resources to these areas. Such a policy has implications which are discussed fully in Chapter 7. Thirdly, there is the scale of resources. This has two effects—(1) given the present low levels of expenditure there is currently a tendency to establish very hard criteria of usefulness which perhaps affect the area of basic research, and (2) as (or if) the levels of expenditure increase, there is some possibility that the demands for more coordination, more centralized decision making about projects and practices, will lead to a 'research policy' for the social sciences and education. This is not an immediate problem (although the post-Rothschild debate might hasten the process of thought) but it is a distinct possibility and is largely the outcome of changes in the market for R & D.

CHAPTER 6

International Experience

Concern for the objectives and organization of educational research is not confined to Great Britain. In most European countries during the period 1955–1970 the resources devoted to education have broadly doubled from three per cent to six per cent of the total government budget. As the outflow of resources has increased, so has the interest in research.

Three main strands account for this interest and all are represented by arrangements within the OECD and the Council of Europe which has done much to encourage such interest. The first factor is the sheer scale of resources devoted to education—and this prompted the establishment of the Study Group in Economics of Education in 1962. This group holds an annual conference, publishes papers, etc. and generally acts as a meeting point to discuss major matters of interest. Thus, in 1963 the famous meeting on the Residual Factor and Economic Growth was held and this has been followed by meetings devoted to the Financing of Education for Economic Growth (1964); Social Objectives in Educational Planning and other similar topics (see references for OECD reports).

The second strand has been the constant concern since the early 1960's over the supply of qualified manpower for the economy. It is widely recognized that one of the objectives of an educational system is the output of qualified manpower, and hence interest was focused on the numbers of scientists and engineers required; the type of education they need; difficulties imposed by the 'swing from science'; and the technical problems associated with manpower forecasting and the relations of manpower supply to regional development, e.g. the Mediterranean regional project. In this the Directorate of Scientific Affairs of OECD has been important.

The third and less clearly defined element in this interest in educational research is concerned with the objectives and utilization of research and the way in which the organization of research can facilitate these objectives. Some tentative steps have been taken towards formulating national reviews of educational policy in member countries with the purpose of clarifying the objectives of educational systems; of achieving more effective allocation of resources between the various sectors of education; of directing research towards those areas which present serious problems; and to relate more closely the results of research and the formulation of policy.

All three factors are important but clearly it is the third element which needs to be discussed at greater length: the relation between research, innovation, the organization of educational research, and the formulation of educational policy.

The starting point is clearly the assessment of resources available for educational research and some account of how they are deployed.

International comparisons are notoriously difficult to make. The collection of data by governments is usually a lengthy undertaking and hence there is often an uneasy compromise between speed of output and accuracy of the results. Definitions of the items under investigation often vary between countries and the periods of time are not always exactly comparable.

Education suffers on nearly all these counts. Naturally, by Education we mean State education—i.e. expenditure by the State on the

TABLE 6.1: *International comparisons of educational R & D*

Country	Year	Total Available for Educational Research	% of Total Educational Expenditure
(1) USA . .	FY 1968	$250 m.	0·31
(2) UK . .	1968/9	£2½–3 m.	0·12
(3) Sweden . .	1970/1	10·4 m. Kronor	0·3 and 0·1
(4) France . .	1968	19·6 m. Fr.	0·09
(5) Netherlands .	1966	10,500,000 Guilder	0·25
(6) UK . .	1968/69	£2·65 m.	0·12

(1) Source: 'Educational R & D in the US'. Committee for Scientific and Technical Research, OECD, 1969. Includes estimates of private foundations ($57 m.); excludes estimates of staff time in universities.

(2) Source: DES estimate prepared for OECD meeting, September 1969—includes staff time at university.

(3) Source: Council of Europe Educational Research Sample Survey 1970, Strasbourg 1971. This figure is somewhat different from the figure given to the OECD meeting, which in 1969/70 was at least 15 m. Kr. The 0·3 per cent indicated above represents research expenditure compared with primary and secondary expenditure. The 0·1 per cent is a comparison of expenditure on and research on higher education (correspondence with Husén and Marklund). Other data give a figure of 8·8 m. Kr. for 1968/9 and a figure of 0·14 per cent.

(4) Source: OECD 1969 meeting. Excludes staff time at university.

(5) Source: OECD 1969 meeting. Excludes staff time at university.

(6) Table 1.4.

public system of education. In some countries, however, the private sector is quite large and to ignore it would be a serious omission in compiling the figure for educational expenditure. The contribution of the private Trusts and Foundations is an important element in a few countries and should be included in research expenditure when making the comparisons of research with total educational expenditure. Again, the items included under 'Education' vary—school transport is a large variable and materials and equipment and capital cost items are significant factors which could make close comparison between countries very difficult. Thus, if the compilation of research expenditure is difficult and the sum of 'total educational expenditure' is difficult the resultant discussion of international comparisons of educational research expenditure is fraught with problems.

Nevertheless, two points are worth discussion: (1) the organization of the research market in different countries, and (2) the identification of problems and policies which seem to be of general international importance.

Two sources of information are generally available which demonstrate clearly the size and nature of the educational research market in other countries. Yates (1971) documents the results of the Unesco Institute of Education Conference of 1967 and summarizes the discussions which took place between participants from fourteen countries. The OECD Directorate of Scientific Affairs has taken a keen interest in educational planning and research and the 1969 meeting led to a major debate on the US system of organizing educational R & D. The results of member countries of surveys of their educational R & D are now available (OECD 1970) and some documentation of active projects is available from the survey conducted by the Council of Europe (1970; 1971). Additional comments from the 1970 Conference on Policies for Educational Growth (OECD 1971) are also relevant.

In almost all countries the state is the sole or overwhelming major supplier of funds either directly through the appropriate ministry or through an array of independent or quasi-independent institutions akin to research councils. The subjects of research are very similar to the results provided earlier: curriculum development, teaching techniques and methods and psychology of learning and teaching. Only the US figures have available a breakdown by sector of education—and in 1968 the US was devoting most funds to early childhood and elementary school sectors. It is likely that the position has altered slightly in three years and that the very low levels of support given to undergraduates and graduate sectors studies has been increased.

Only in the US and UK are private trusts and foundations a significant source of funds—and even here it contributes only about

10 per cent—20 per cent of the total 1968 appropriations. The state is everywhere the main sponsor.

The 'performers' overseas are broadly similar to those in this country: a few universities and a few independent research organizations are the major performers of educational research. Two differences may be noted. In a number of countries—France, Sweden, Japan and developing countries such as Zambia and Thailand, government departments are major performers of educational research. In other countries such as the US the research institutes are financed wholly by the State but are attached to universities and are operated by university staff. Secondly, the relations between educational research and government administration are much closer in many other countries than they are in the UK or US.

As an example of this and as a means of developing the points made above, some discussion of the position in France and the USA seems a useful task, together with some notes on Swedish experience. The points to be stressed are: (1) the relations between sponsors (the State) and performers and (2) the relations between the production of knowledge and the dissemination of results to users. In short, the relations between the objectives of educational R & D and the organization of R & D can be traced by analysing the components of the R & D market and establishing the priorities within the market. This comparison is aided by the substantial uniformity between OECD countries in that all have a low absolute and relative level of expenditure on educational R & D and the pattern of expenditure is broadly similar. Naturally, there are also differences.

This is most marked when one considers the organization of educational research and the sharpest contrast can be made by looking at the French and US institutional arrangements. In France, there are a very few highly centralized and Paris-orientated research centres which can be contrasted with the enormous number, range, type and geographical spread of institutions in the USA.

French educational research was enlarged and reorganized in 1964 and 1967 by the creation of units at the Ministry of Education for the support and encouragement of R & D. The projects were mainly concerned with Development rather than Research and not until 1969/70 was a central body established to plan and coordinate research as well as development work. The Comité da la Recherche et du Développement de l'Education Nationale is composed entirely of Ministry personnel and, although other members can be co-opted, there is no *de jure* representative of research either from the universities or elsewhere. Such centralization of R & D certainly secures the very close relation of sponsored work to policy formation and, given the scarcity of research workers and the recent interest in

R & D, it is perhaps understandable that control should be exercised so centrally.

This centralization of all development work is in sharp contrast to the diffuseness of basic research efforts. Sponsors and users operate quite independently of each other—particularly the main two units—the Ministry of Education and the Délégation Général à la Recherche Scientifique et Technique (DGRST) and the non-State performers who are a loose group of universities and specialist institutes such as Institut Pédagogique National (IPN) and Institut National de Statistique et des Etudes Economiques (INSEE).

The effects of central control over development and the rather loose coordination of research are not easily assessed. One suspects that research priorities are chosen by individual researchers without regard to some overview of what is most 'valuable'. It is probable that the sponsor and users, because of the weak links, have as yet to determine the balance both between R & D and within each category.

There can be little doubt, however, that the central control of funds —and Paris orientated institutional performers—can and probably does stifle development work. For almost all research and development projects decisions on funding are taken at a national, i.e. ministerial level, before work can proceed. In short, for all long-term reasonable scale projects which require external financing—and this means nearly all development and applied research—decisions are governed by the government departments' requirements. The notable exception is the Centre National pour la Recherche Scientifique (CNRS). This is a large, autonomous bureau type organization which has its own research funds and is well equipped to pursue longer-term work. Relatively little of the work is educational research although some work is related to the education system and learning behaviour.

The notable features of the French system then are the contrast between highly centralized development with applied, policy-orientated research work and the diffuse unco-ordinated basic research conducted at the universities. Until the CRDEN is broadened in membership and establishes guidelines for R & D financing it is difficult to see any fruitful relationship emerging between the basic work which is carried on in the universities and the policy-orientated research and development performed at the IPN and elsewhere. The benefits of educational research seem to flow directly to policy makers on the one hand and to the academic world of learning on the other. Teachers and others within the educational system—who in any case are educated and trained in different (non-university) sectors of higher education must find it very difficult to understand and improve the educational development of the pupils. More hope but perhaps little real expectation must be given to the Centres Régionaux de Documentation Pédagogique which devote much effort to the retaining of teachers. The final points to be drawn from the discussion of the French experience are the shortage of well-trained, experienced research staff, the low absolute and relative levels of finance and the poor channels of dissemination. This could have been drawn from the experiences of almost any country (see Yates, 1971; OECD papers 1971), but it completes the picture of French experience in organizing educational R & D.

In the USA the position is radically different. Every effort is made to secure maximum geographical coverage and to involve as many teachers and schools as possible in R & D projects. There is an enormous array of institutional arrangements designed to secure this objective. The main basic research effort is located in the universities and is largely unco-ordinated and only partially funded. Much of the work is located in bureaux, institutes, etc. attached to the schools and departments of education, but as the attention of the social and behavioural sciences is drawn towards education, more work is coming from the direction of departments of sociology, psychology and others.

Much R & D is now increasingly located in the new institutions created in the past decade. There are nine R & D centres (as at 1969) which have been established gradually at various universities since the enabling Act of 1963. The Office of Education allocates the funds, receives the R & D programme and evaluates results. The objectives of the centres are to bridge research, development, and diffusion; to close gaps between research and practice; and to advise and guide school-based R & D and generally to offer expertise to the interested groups—teachers, supervisors, principals, and other school-based personnel.

Each R & D centre receives about $1m p.a. and draws its staff from the universities and elsewhere. There tend to be some specialisms—early childhood AV-Institution, educational administration—and the centres, of course, are very big by university department, or even bureau, research standards—perhaps three times the average bureau size (see Chase, 1970).

Not everything is successful—the university departments are a little disturbed about the nature and standard of the work; the allocation criteria for awarding grants is not always clear; and the evaluation element in the programme has been criticised. Perhaps the most significant criticism, however, lies in the academic status attached to basic rather than developmental research work and the natural scepticism accorded to middlemen in industrialized societies. Middlemen have never been well respected, presumably because the functions they perform, although important, can be seen a parasitic—the transmission of goods and ideas from one set of institutions/persons to another set. This is expensive and sometimes risky and premium/profits are often generous. Hence the suspicions of middlemen (see Chase, 1970).

R & D centres are intended to act as middlemen and have been uncertain as to the relative importance of different aspects of their task. To gain respectability and status they must operate on some basic research. To gain the admiration of the schools they must engage in innovation and school-based development work. To satisfy, or be accountable to, the USOE they must successfully demonstrate that the research and development functions can be integrated with innovation in the schools. Time is the crucial element in this enterprise and it is ironic that evaluation of the centres is instant, continuous, rather hostile, and comes at a time when they have been operating at something like full strength for less than five years. The signs are that USOE funding is running out and may not be renewed (in the financial year 1973) and there is every likelihood that much interesting work will be abandoned (see *Educational Researcher*, December 1970).

Perhaps the main reason for this is the absence of precise specification of objectivity by the USOE and the evaluation of the results emerging from R & D centres. Equally, there has been the academic insistence on freedom to pursue their own ideas and policies, which for both personal and professional reasons are likely to turn towards the research end of the Research→Development→Innovation spectrum. There is also the very real problem of evaluation techniques. Not only is the evaluation/research/service argument still extant (Witrock and Wiley, 1971), but there is also the disenchantment with current evaluation methods (ability) to reveal any significant differences in instructional methods, reallocation of resources, or other interventions in the educational system (Stufflebeam *et al.*, 1971).

It is difficult to gauge attitudes towards the Regional Educational Laboratories (RELs). They were established after the R & D centres as part of the amendments to the Elementary and Secondary Education (ESEA) Act of 1965. By 1969 over 30 RELs were operating. 'They are school orientated; innovation and dissemination orientated' and 'charged with the task of making R & D results apply to the schools', as the USOE rather richly phrase it (OECD, 1969). Most of them specialize in one or two fields and nearly all include teacher involvement or teacher retraining as part of their functions. 'The development of the network of REL was guided by the understanding that no single existing institution was strategically located or empowered to relate effectively all segments of the educational community whose involvement was necessary to produce educational change through educational development throughout the highly decentralized US school system. The judgement was made that a new institution was required to stimulate a powerful educational partnership of individuals and agencies with a wide variety of judicial responsibilities to tie R & D more closely to the improvement of instructional practice' (OECD, 1969).

There is a reasonably broad base to the operations: they do not restrict the R & D work within too narrow limits and a wide range of work overlaps with the R & D centres. However, they face serious difficulties: they are in direct competition with the university departments, institutes and bureaux, the R & D centres, and the State-operated research units. The career tenure of RELs is very uncertain and hence staff are not perhaps of the highest calibre.

Again, RELs are expected to produce 'results'. They were deliberately designed to be inventive, to apply results in the schools; insofar as they are successful they satisfy the schools and the USOE, but 'they inevitably attract the antagonism of those States who believe that R & D ought to figure more prominently in the State Department of Education' (OECD, 1969), and they are further divorced from the traditional orientation of universities. As the examiners comment, 'opinion about the RELs differ . . . the judgements however seem to depend primarily upon what criteria are being applied . . . .It is then upon them that the heaviest burden of proof will fall. If anything useful is to appear in the schools from all of the research efforts it will, presumably, be mediated through the REL more than any other single group or institution' (see also Taylor, 1972; and the discussion by Bloom 1968; Boyan, 1969; and Chase 1970).

It is unfortunate that this reaction to the optimistic view of the mid-1960s should be so severe and that the chastened mood of research workers should coincide with the strong scepticism of administrators, determined that R & D expenditure should be made accountable in the same way as other public expenditure.

This has been a major recent development which has parallelled the growth of performance contracting and the public demand for 'educational accountability'. Accountability is another portmanteau word that covers a range of activities such as assessment, evaluation, budgeting and financial control and performance contracting. The theory and practice of programming planning and budgeting derives from the USA (particularly the US Government and specifically in defence contracting) and is now widely applied to school districts (see Hartley, 1968). Evaluation, of course, has an enormous literature, much of which has been generated by the universities, the R & D Centres and the RELs within the last decade. Much of the most interesting work lies in integrating the cost analysis and resource planning activities with educational evaluation and some preliminary work is available which could set guidelines in the UK (see Stufflebeam *et al.*, 1971; Wittrock and Wiley [Eds.] 1970).

Performance contracting is relatively new and can be seen as a much 'harder' attempt to achieve accountability. In essence a subject or topic area is contracted out to an educational and/or publishing company which guarantees that all children will achieve agreed performance standards after following a prescribed course. The company, of course, is paid a fee for the contract which is not payable (in part or in full) if the children fail to meet the standards (see Spaght, 1971). It is recognized that performance cannot really be 'guaranteed'; it is also recognized that there is a limited amount of data available for many of the topics. Finally, it is the case that performance contracting makes more sense for innovative programmes than for traditional subjects and techniques. Companies are unlikely to risk resources in the preparation of traditional textbooks—but for new learning systems there is a good prospect of extending sales if the expertize of the company can be employed to show (if not guarantee) improved results. The range of contracts is limited and the resources involved are quite small—perhaps two-and-a-half per cent of the schools educational budget—(Educational Testing Service, 1971), but the pressures from the public and school administrators are likely to extend this form of instruction (Davis, 1971). This is certainly true of the hardware based systems and the 'new' learning systems produced by publishing companies and the suppliers of educational technology. However, at present it is just a part of the general pressure for accountability in the USA. Such pressures are developing here in the UK and it is interesting to note a recent SSRC grant to a Leeds College to investigate the effects of subcontracting learning systems to independent companies.

It is the insistence on dissemination, innovation and adoption mechanism that perhaps distinguishes the US R & D effort from other countries. Much of the concern of the USOE has been to 'improve practice' and of course the insistence on accountability makes dissemination and innovation attractive areas for allocating funds. The obvious example is the Educational Research Information Centre (ERIC) and the work of the RELs. The success of ERIC is already assured. The sheer volume of sales recorded in the 1965–1969 period (OECD, 1969) should demonstrate success. It is clearly a vital point of any R & D effort. Research and reports, abstracts of articles, bibliographies, microfiche copies of theses, reports, etc. are indispensible to any study of a topic or problem. ERIC informs, and thereby avoids duplication, encourages relevant replication and effective decision making at school, university, State and technical level. At the same time, the participants at the Unesco conference seemed unable to find many examples of the research→invention→innovation→adoption model. 'In most cases the invention neither originated in basic research studies, nor was it the subject of research during its development. In no case could appreciable research evidence about its effectiveness be offered by those recommending its adoption. Some practices have been made the subject of empirical study after the fact and a great many of the findings have been inconclusive and conflicting. Such findings have had no appreciable effort on public or professional allegiance to the practice' (Yates, 1971). It is true that research findings can be traced that would support, modify, or encourage the use of certain procedures in the USA—indeed, a few examples were given but it illustrates the weak links between R & D and adoption of innovations in the country which probably devotes more attention to this problem than most. If the US effort is relatively weak it is likely that most other countries have yet to concern themselves with models and mechanisms for relating R & D, dissemination and innovation (see the discussion about Sweden in Yates, 1971; OECD, 1969; also Havelock *et al*, 1969).

Some tentative conclusions

This brief account of educational research experience in other countries allows one to conclude that there is a large measure of shared experience. All countries have a level of funding below 0·5 per cent of total educational expenditure; in all countries, the Government is the main supplier of funds either directly through the Education Ministries, or indirectly through councils, bureaux, or institutes; and in most countries much of the research is undertaken at universities, although the importance of bureaux or institutes with full-time research workers is to be stressed, as is the importance of Ministry-based research work.

The interesting variation is the degree of control exercised within the organizational framework. There is no clear and obvious explanation for differences in the organization. Tradition is probably important—the centralist *v* local habit in the educational system is likely to be perpetuated in any R & D organization. No doubt inertia is also important: until one reflects on the objectives of the organization it is difficult to decide rationally on the 'best' organization to establish and hence the arrangements for educational research are simply established piecemeal and develop as and when they can.

The interesting point is to reconsider the objectives of educational research and reflect on the type of establishment which is most likely to achieve those objectives. This will serve to draw together the fragmentary results of this discussion of international experience and will introduce the next chapter's work on research policy, planning and innovation.

Educational research serves multiple purposes. It advances knowledge—of, say, learning and teaching theory; it forms the basis of new methods, techniques and curricula; it studies policy problems, e.g. school leaving age, and educational organization. In short, the benefits of educational research flow to both the academic world and the school and classroom; and to the policy makers—central and local government officials. Given the different objectives, it is not surprising that different organizational patterns exist. The major difference in organization seems to stem from the weighting/importance of these three major objectives. No country deliberately encourages advances in knowledge at the expense of the other two areas—this indeed is one of the difficulties, and hence organizational variation depends on the relative importance attached to school-based knowledge, policy-orientated research, and the traditional work of the universities.

In the USA attention has been paid to improving the schools, and a regional organization has been created. This deliberate attempt to decentralize the R & D effort seems partially successful, although it is rather too early to evaluate 'success' except in terms of expressed approval of the arrangements by school board supervisors, and the USOE.

The distinctive feature of this organization is the direct involvement of teachers and school staff, and the intention to relate research work to the training and retraining of teachers. This has been much neglected by most other countries, including the UK, and has resulted in much indifference and a little hostility between researcher and teacher. Yet if one of the main objectives of educational research is the improvement of school and classroom performance it is foolish to alienate the teachers. To include them within the organization of educational research seems logical and is a necessary, albeit not sufficient, step to ensure good working relationships. There is still the old dilemma—how to reorganize teacher training so that the teachers are receptive to the aims and methods of researchers and at the same time ensure that the R & D work is relevant to teaching needs. There are many practical problems involved in this reoganization but Michael Young (1965) has argued that research and innovation need to be far more closely related and Stephen Wiseman has aptly remarked that one of the most serious constraints on research work is the co-operation of schools and teachers (Wiseman, 1973). Involvement may produce cooperation.

One can perhaps generalize the point and argue that the closer relationship of research work and teacher education (including retraining and in-service courses) is a pre-requisite of effective innovation in schools. The gap between research and innovation in the schools sector of education lies in the current absence of teacher involvement in research. To close the gap, to develop the theory and practice of research→innovation→adoption models, it is necessary to reorganize teacher education and to adopt an action-orientated approach to educational research.

This of course is to give prominence to the 'improvement of educational instruction' objective of educational R & D. There is little new in this view (Young, 1965) but one can now point to US, French and other attempts to relate research and development work to school instruction.

To make the point more general one may conclude that there is a clear case for integrating research work and the teaching profession in the interests of improving educational instruction. This satisfies one objective of educational research; it would be welcomed by the colleges of education; the organization structure would require thought (see Taylor, 1972); and of course the resources and institutions would need to be made available. It seems that one must rely more on hope than expectation that teacher education and research work will be more closely related as a means of turning the research→innovation→adoption models into practice.

In other countries the policy objectives of educational R & D seem to be regarded as more important. This seems to be true of France and to some extent of Sweden, and this preference or priority for one set of objectives rather than others is reflected in the more centralized organization of sponsors and performers.

In both countries the performers are closely placed to government departments both physically and by the lines of communication which exist between sponsors and performers. The emphasis on policy-orientated studies has certain implications both for the organization of educational research and the pattern of research work. In France, as has been seen, the volume of R & D work is quite small and is closely geared to the requirements of the Ministry of Education. The research elsewhere is confined to the universities and is unrelated to the research and development effort pursued at the Ministry and other central research organizations. In Sweden, too, there are relatively few research institutions and the sponsorship is confined to the two central Government institutions—the National Board for Education and the Office of the Chancellor of the Swedish

Universities. In addition, there is a Social Science Research Council which has independent control of an additional allocation of State funds. It is true that the working relations between the authorities and researchers in the Planning and Research Bureau of the Ministry are very good—but the research work is quite deliberately orientated to current policy problems. As this is balanced by the more basic work sponsored by the SSRC, there is no real problem of misallocation or uneven distribution of research effort which could otherwise—as in France—be a difficulty of this form of organization.

Another difficulty which can arise from insistence on the policy-making objectives of educational research is the restricted flow of information. It is not surprising that decision makers and administrators wish to formulate policy in private if not in secret. Despite the call for more 'openness' in decision making (Fulton Report, Great Britain, Civil Service, 1968) it is true not only of the British civil service, but of most bureaucracies that decision making should be undertaken with the minimum amount of noise, public debate and other 'interference'. The publication of information which could (or should) be available to aid decision making is therefore likely to be delayed, restricted, edited or otherwise controlled and this can only be undesirable. Research results should be widely circulated to the academic, professional and all other sectors of the community. It is also relevant to note that R & D can only be optimised if policy problems (or any other problems) are perceived, discussed and formulated in researchable terms. If policy making continues to be 'closed' rather than 'open' it is unlikely that R & D can be fully effective.

Finally, there is the more general point that a climate of policy orientated research leads to the insistence on relevance as the main criterion for awarding research funds. This is a natural attitude for Government departments to adopt but it has a limiting effect on R & D work if the balance of sponsors' funds is unevenly distributed between the various types of R & D work in response to the competing demands to serve different objectives of R & D. As usual, the problem is not one of intentions but of resources: if more resources were available no doubt both objectives could be satisfied. It is however a real fact that resource allocation to educational research is so limited that the direction of funds towards certain objectives must seriously affect the amount of work possible in other areas. Hence the concern—expressed at most international conferences—over the balance of policy-orientated and basic/academic/school-orientated work.

In the UK there has been little reflection on the objectives and related organization of educational research so that the resulting pattern is hard to characterize. The DES is concerned with policy-orientated work; the Schools Council concentrates on teachers, schools and improved instruction objectives; the SSRC operates in the more basic research end of the market. The other sponsors have—and exercise—considerable freedom in the choice of projects to fund. In principle this is a reasonably balanced effort; in practice the performer is constrained by the sponsor's criterion of relevance which is not always clearly identified, and it is not at all clear that the market allocates funds efficiently.

It is possible that, although the total volume of R & D may remain much the same, the market is being short circuited by sponsors and the resulting research work may not reflect performers' preferences. If the criterion of relevance is extended and applied rigorously—particularly in the field of policy-orientated work—then the volume of R & D funds available to the rest of the market may contract and the information flows may be curtailed, because sponsors find it more convenient, if not more efficient, to perform work themselves.

The gist of this discussion, then, is that the international experience of educational R & D and its organization is closely parallel to the UK experience. Some points have been drawn from this account but a more detailed discussion of the policies and problems within the R & D market is needed and this is provided in the final chapter.

CHAPTER 7

Policies and Problems in Educational Research and Development

Introduction

The costs of educational R & D have been detailed in previous chapters. One can briefly repeat here that about £2m p.a. of externally funded R & D work is performed in England and Wales, together with an additional £500,000 p.a. made available through the universities. What is now required is an extended account of the benefits case for educational R & D funds; the problems of formulating a policy for educational R & D; and finally, some discussion of the utilization of research output with special attention to the various models which relate the research/development/dissemination and innovation process.

The case for R & D

It is rather surprising to discover that so little attention has been paid to making a case for research and development in education. There is of course the early address by Wall (1959) and the symposium at Manchester organized by the BPS addressed by Wall (1962) and Wiseman (1962) but there was a general tacit assumption that more resources for educational R & D would be desirable and attention was focused more on the problems of using extra resources than as the rationale for demanding additional funds. It is surprisingly difficult to make a case for more R & D. Each of the three main planks in the argument contain serious difficulties and one is left finally with the argument advanced by Chase (1969 and 1970).

The user demand argument

The first case must be the argument from consumer demand: that the users of R & D are urging further inquiries and studies into problems that they find important and urgent. In fact, it is a well known phenomenon that practitioners and administrators within the educational system are in many ways the least active supporters of the R & D market. On the one hand, teachers seem to have little knowledge and use for research results and, on the other hand, policy makers are very weak supporters of R & D because, even when results are available, either the information channels are so poor that knowledge is not transmitted or the information cannot be used without modification and there are few links (consultancies) that can bridge the administrative gap between decision making and the utilization of R & D information. It is therefore rare to find direct links between research results and policy decisions. The reasons are quite well known (Yates, 1971; Cane & Schroeder, 1971). There is a lack of communication between research staff, teachers, and administrators which prevents the free flow of information; there is the great problem of 'relevance' which those performing research often fail to recognize and those who use results often cannot grasp that research cannot usually produce unequivocal guides to practice but must be utilized carefully with full knowledge of its uncertainty and imperfections; and, finally, there is the very real problem of the different orientations of the component groups in the R & D market. This is often brushed aside as a minor problem but the failure to understand and cooperate with associate groups is a well-documented phenomenon in industry and administration and is accorded an important place in any explanation of poor working relations, inefficient practices and low productivity (Higgins and Jessop, 1965). Whatever the reasons, there is an unsatisfactory relation between the performers and users of R & D work, and if the education service fails to use the results of research it is very difficult to avoid the conclusion that education can find little rationale for increased funds from this quarter.

The economic return argument

The case for more R & D resources cannot then depend on user demand, and one must turn to the argument from usefulness, productivity and 'positive returns' to research. There are two products or outputs obtainable from the R & D process—advances in knowledge and information which can be used directly or indirectly in the teaching and policy making situations and the possibility of a process or product invention. It is not at all clear that R & D in the social sciences produces 'inventions' or any analogue of invention as it is recognized in the natural sciences. Perhaps audio-visual techniques, programmed instruction, learning systems, school organization patterns, processes of budgetary control and so on are inventions in some sense. If so, then they may be direct results of R & D and they could be counted as a good reason for finding the returns to R & D to be positive.

On balance, it is likely that many in education would hold the view that invention and innovation are largely independent of research work although some development work may be necessary. There is a fairly clear distinction (to repeat Lazarfeld and Sieber, 1964) between understanding the educational process and system and the improvement of the system. Most *users* of R & D work are interested in the latter view and hence development funds may be justified but research resources are difficult to support. Such a view is also held in the physical sciences (Jewkes *et al.*, 1969; Nelson, 1959a) but the steady stream of argument over basic *v* applied work and their relative attributes and contributions to growth and efficiency does little to resolve the problem.

There is some direct evidence that educational R & D has contributed significantly to improved productivity and effectiveness within the educational system. One thinks naturally of the major research studies on early childhood which surrounded the Plowden report; of the work of i.t.a. and other reading methods; of the early work at the NFER on IQ tests as well as reading and maths achievement tests; and the range of work on re-thinking curricula and teaching methods encouraged by the Nuffield Foundation and the Schools Council. As indicated earlier, higher education as a sector involving 18+ selection, university finances and student/manpower forecasting are also notable areas of research activity following the Robbins report. Without this stream of information it is likely that policies and decisions would be even more *ad hoc* and hesitant than they have been. Although forecasts and analysis may be imperfect, they do reveal the existence of a problem area and indicate the complexity of the topic. Decisions must therefore be contingent on change and anticipated change rather than follow desperately in the wake of existing problems. There will, no doubt, always be some element of crisis management; but it is one of the tasks of R & D to anticipate future development and feed information to administrators in an attempt to forestall change (Taylor, 1970).

The economic value of information

If it is somewhat rare to find direct application of R & D work, it is important to trace the various ways in which information is disseminated and used by practitioners and administrators. This problem is not peculiar to education—it affects the social sciences generally—and must be applicable to any rationale for arts and social science research funds. The point is critical because information is the major output from the R & D process.

Dissemination problems are legion—there are relatively few channels for administrators and decision makers at national and local levels and the channels to practitioners are of very varying quality. If the quantitative and qualitative difficulties of obtaining information are compounded with the motives and attitudes frequently held by practitioners and administrators, it is not surprising that the information and knowledge 'gap' is as large as it is. It is the utilization of information that is both important and interesting. Riecken (1969) identifies three obstacles to the application of social science information to social problems: (1) the manipulability of variables; (2) the Hawthorne effect; and (3) the defects of available data. Much theoretical work, he argues, uses variables such as early childhood experience, or sex, or father's occupation. Alternatively, explanations are given in terms such as the attitudes of the teacher or the social background or school-home relationhips which are too large and undifferentiated. A policy maker requires a variable which can be controlled such that intervention in the social or educational scene can be attempted. The use of information based on fixed variables such as age or sex cannot really help, nor are the undifferentiated variables much use as policy aids. The Hawthorne effect is well known but is still a serious constraint to the administrator: how does one differentiate between change induced by one variable and changes in other variables surrounding the experimental conditions?

Indirect or incomplete data are perhaps the most serious difficulties facing those in social science research. In most cases, government-collected data (apart from social book-keeping data) are not readily available to researchers. Data are therefore a prior necessity of most educational research—and the forms and methods of collection are well known to be suspect. Survey work, interviews, etc., all depend on the memory, attitudes and behaviour of the individuals and omissions and errors are a natural consequence of such data gathering exercises. There are technical answers to some of these difficulties but one must accept the basic problem of incomplete data. Given this, there is further reason for the users to doubt the usefulness of educational research results.

Utilizing information

The difficulties of utilizing research are severe. The most obvious problem is that the products are so intangible. 'Information' may take the form of an idea, practices, policies, routines or even such vague data as knowledge of attitudes and opinions. It is hard for users to feel much confidence in such intangibles compared with 'inventions' and 'concepts' which are also products of R & D. Even if they did act on such information it is not clear what success would be achieved or how one would measure such success. Practices and motives in education and social behaviour are harder to teach and learn than comparable advances in knowledge in the physical sciences: there is a direct requirement to adjust social relationships in order for the changed attitudes, routines, etc., to operate effectively; and such change is not only long term but involves variables other than the one under consideration. Thus, changes in reading practices usually involve reorganizing primary school classrooms; have an impact on other curricula features; and can change staff–children relations. One of the reasons that economic research is reasonably successful in its transmission from theory to utilization is that so little social change is needed. The economic mechanisms of the marketing system and fiscal system are already there (subject to small-scale changes) and the policies can be adopted without major personal and institutional changes. Educational change is much slower, more fundamental and difficult than this, and therefore the relations between research and educational change are far more diffuse and less easily perceived.

One of the most interesting aspects of utilizing social science results is the mechanism for developing 'inventions' into marketable (useable) products. A real problem here is that the market must almost always be the State. In most social situations the products partake of all the characteristics of 'public goods' (see Margolis and Guitton, 1970). Thus, the inventor is unable to appropriate the benefits of invention (except in prestige or other non-market benefits) and the market mechanism for translating social inventions into innovation and use are almost non-existent. Only in a few cases—curricula materials, personnel selection and testing, printed or visual aids—is there a commercial market for R & D results. In most other cases the mechanisms for transmitting results to users are political. It is the 'system'—local or national—that must be persuaded that new practices, processes, methods must be introduced and this process of innovation and adoption is ill understood. If to his research skills the R & D man must add political skills and marketing flair there seems little hope for major utilization of R & D results.

One obvious reason for the lack of a private market is of course that most social science 'inventions' cannot be valued. When this is recognized and added to the fact that it is in the public sector that any innovations must be introduced it is no surprise that the State must act as its own marketing mechanism. It is in this sense that social science information can be—and is—used by administrators. They have to make decisions, allocate resources, and make judgements. How useful the corporate body of social science knowledge can be in these practices is a point perhaps best summed up by Riecken (1969): 'The physical and biological sciences encounter problems of over-utilization or careless utilization or premature application while the parallel discussion in the social sciences mostly turns out to be complaints about non-utilization' (see reply in Dror and Plowman, 1970).

Improving the utilization of information

There is no reason to suppose that this is likely to be a permanent state of affairs nor that efforts are not being made to improve the utilization of R & D results. The signs of change are obvious and improvements in mechanisms are slow but are being established.

There is, of course, the recognized need for sponsors and performers to establish the general and specific objectives of the research much more closely before the work is under way. Much of the disappointment expressed by sponsors seems due to misunderstanding of the activities of the research teams and/or for not clarifying and insisting on work on their (the sponsors) interests. 'In general, executive agencies—such as the Office of Education, the Public Health Office—can be faulted for not communicating sufficiently clear and limited goals' (Orlans, 1968). Bureaucracy likes broad goals because it 'renders a failure serious enough to endanger survival unlikely and difficult to identify, and allows a posture flexible enough to adopt to changing circumstances and political realities' (Orlans, 1968, p. 153). Similarly, scientists like broad goals because it simplifies the process of accommodating professional and personal interests. If broad goals make it difficult to prove failure they also make it difficult to identify success and deny triviality and irrelevance. It is to be hoped that these lessons have been learned and that research work will have more clearly defined objectives capable of attainment.

There is also the enormous importance which has been placed on evaluation. The use of evaluation seems a prime candidate for sponsors' attentions: the work is clearly useful, it is fairly readily defineable and achievable—it is one area where the degree of uncertainty seems low—and in principle it would seem that the results could be applied directly. The obstacles to good evaluation work are quite well known (Wiseman and Pidgeon, 1970; Wittock and Wiley 1970; Stufflebeam *et al.*, 1971). There is often the need for political commitment to a programme *before* evaluation can commence and it is then difficult to see what difference the research results would have on the policy. Where evaluation does take place with small pilot studies the results are open to doubt and in education the 'no significant difference' finding begins to cast doubt on the techniques themselves. This is the main point which Guba (1969) makes in his distinction between research and evaluation. 'The classic research paradigm is not the paradigm of evaluation, not can it ever be. . . . Research is not the same as evaluation and the sooner we recognize that fact the better off we all will be'.

Despite this outburst there is some general acknowledgement of the need for more (and better) evaluation. The Rand Corporation is the usual paradigm or model taken—where, although much of the work is confidential to Washington there is much externally published work made available and the 'independent' status of Rand at least implies some confidence in those reports on Government activity that are published. In some ways the weakness of the civil bureaucracy can be made good by the determination of Congress—the famous Coleman report, on equality of educational opportunity, is a good example. . . . 'If the USOE had not been able to use Congress as the bearer of ultimate responsibility the research would not have been carried out and instead a very weak and non-controversial report would have resulted'. (Coleman quoted in Orlans, 1968).

The mechanisms for innovation are also changing. The SSRC have had an Academic Liaison Officer system for some time: there is a similar network of third persons operating in industry; and the awareness of the need for in-service courses, re-education and use of available and new knowledge is growing rapidly. There is also much concern for the methods by which innovations develop from basic research and the subsequent diffusion of innovations (Havelock, 1969; Carlson, 1965).

In conclusion, then, there are, on balance, positive returns to educational R & D (and social science generally) despite the obstacles to the production, dissemination and utilization of R & D results. Educational (social science) R & D is indispensible to national action by public and private institutions. It is an essential element in the evaluation of local and national programmes for education, to the appropriate allocation of resources and to intelligent decision making. Indeed it is argued later that information as an aid to decision making is one of the main benefits. The use of economic and psychological research is well documented: educational research is equally essential in the formulation and execution of educational and welfare policies and practice. One must improve, not abandon, the use of research data within the educational system, in an attempt to make educational practice and decision-making more effective.

The knowledge base argument

If one is still doubtful as to the value of R & D then one can only be persuaded by the argument from growth and improvement through knowledge. There are two aspects to this argument.

The first area is associated with Wall (1959) and Wiseman (1962): and relies on the intuitive common sense view that '. . . any service which accounts for £2400m each year, employs or occupies nearly 30 per cent of the population; and accounts for almost half of the activities of local government in the country must surely require more than £3m p.a. to examine, diagnose and inform its objectives and operations' (Wall, 1959).

A more extensive rationale is provided by Chase (1969 and 1971). He takes note of the 'knowledge explosion' and the remarkable growth in rate and directions of social and economic change in the past two or three decades. He then argues in a penetrating passage that: 'Observation of the current scene seems to indicate that the most dynamic and effective operations in our society rely heavily on continuing inputs of knowledge relevant to the enterprise, and the speedy application of new knowledge to the solution of problems and the attainment of objectives. A corollary is that occupations and enterprises which operate from a weak knowledge base, or which falter in their efforts to adapt knowledge and technology to their special requirements, operate at a serious disadvantage. Few can doubt that education is in this category. Although proclaimed without audible dissent as one of the enterprises most crucial to our society, it has poor access to knowledge-producing and knowledge-applying resources. Consequently, it exhibits a low capacity for generating new knowledge; its development is not closely linked to research; and its practitioners receive inadequate help in translating substantive, theoretical, and technological knowledge into educational operations' (Chase, 1970).

This must be the main ground on which the case for R & D in education and the social sciences must rest: there is a need for information about the educational system and the weakness of current efforts to produce and utilize such information must be a spur to increase rather than diminish the resources devoted to R & D. This concludes the benefits of—or the case for—educational R & D. It is difficult to demonstrate quantitatively that benefits exceed costs: indeed it is one of the areas which is overdue for examination. It is, however, beyond reasonable doubt that if the knowledge industry is itself so weak in the production of information about itself then the benefits of such an examination must be substantial.

The formulation of a policy for research

A model of the R & D market was discussed in Chapter 5. It was argued that the traditional passive model is gradually changing in the face of at least three identified pressures. It is the implications of a research policy which are perhaps the most important aspects of change and certainly the point which has the most interesting economic and administrative implications. The formulation of a policy seems to imply a remarkable faith in the ability of the R & D market to respond to fluctuations in resources. It relies on the improved assumption that increased expenditure will yield increases in results which seems to suffer from at least two major difficulties discussed later.

The movement towards a research policy as suggested by SSRC is tentative, inconclusive and by no means generally acceptable to members: as the SSRC's 1969/70 Report puts it, 'to make the simple transition from the identification of a number of urgent issues of social policy to a comprehensive plan of research to solve one after another of the many problems that beset the policymaker . . . is beguiling to some and wholly distasteful to others'.

The end product may well be despair or disappointment: for as another SSRC Report puts it, 'It is not so much a matter of an ordered hierarchy of priorities as a process of grasping at opportunities presented by an almost accidental coagulation of interests among a group of able research workers around some chosen problem in order to shift the frontier of knowledge forward' (SSRC 1970/1 Report).

There is a deal of difference between the matching of sponsors' 'needs' and researchers' interests—however accidental—and the deliberate attempt to cultivate some areas to the exclusion of others by means of a 'rational' research policy. The implication and problem of such a policy needs to be considered carefully.

Implications of a research policy

The basic premises of such a policy are:

(1) that general recognition of the need to research in the selected subject/topic areas will be obtained from both the academic and administrative/policy worlds;

(2) that able research workers will come forward with well designed programmes to fulfil these tasks;

(3) that the probability of success is high, i.e. that uncertainty of the outcomes will be carefully calculated;

(4) that communications within the R & D field are efficient in order to avoid duplication and misunderstanding, and to ensure good matching of researcher and sponsor;

(5) that investment in these areas after allowances for (2) and (3) will yield a higher return than alternative policies.

In short, the formulation of a research policy takes the view that the R & D market will respond in a manner similar to other economic markets: that is by raising the price or rewards researchers will come forward and work in the field—and will be successful. It also assumes that increases in inputs will generate increases in output.

It may be that the knowledge market is different fundamentally from other markets, in precisely these respects. On the one hand many research workers are creative people and are motivated by intellectual interests rather than by the presence of gaps in 'our' knowledge (with 'our') to be filled: only if a 'coagulation of interests' exists is good research work likely to be developed. On the other hand, nothing is certain about research outcomes except their uncertainty. These two areas deserve further comment.

The objectives of performers

The motivations, personality, and creativity of research workers have been the objects of study for the past two decades or more—and we know relatively little about the area. The stimulus to inquiry was primarily the study of 'creativity'—the identification and measurement of the attribute. Naturally, it was thought that creativity should be exhibited by scientists and a number of studies of creativity used scientists as case material. Another stimulus to the inquiry was the economic importance of research and development work in industry; which of course is primarily scientific and technological R & D—again, therefore, scientific inquiries formed part of the samples.

The striking point from this research (Taylor and Barron, 1963; Mackinnon, 1962) is that most research scientists employed in industrial R & D are primarily motivated by non-economic values. Even inventors place financial rewards below curiosity (Rossman, 1931). The urge to find theoretical problems and to solve them with elegance and finesse is of much greater significance: it is what has been called elsewhere the green-grass syndrome (Taylor and Barron, 1963) which extends to studies of R & D organizations and to the values/opinions of directors of research establishments.

The implications, therefore, must be that sponsors who set guidelines, policies, and strategies for research groups, and direct work into certain areas rather than others should first find researchers willing and able to work in those areas. If the major drives are intellectual interest then one is dependent on finding a 'coagulation of interests': without it one finds either second-best researchers who have few ideas of their own or inexperienced workers willing to learn on any project but who leave as they become more interested in other work.

In educational research the position is somewhat different from that in the natural sciences. Firstly, we do not have any studies of researchers which could confirm the view that research workers share the same characteristics and values as their scientific colleagues. It may therefore be misleading to argue that researchers will or will not be motivated to work in those areas were funds are made available. Secondly, it is not clear what constitutes a research output in educational research. If we look for the equivalent of basic science then we perhaps want research workers who are different from the inventor. From previous discussions it is probable that the balance of research effort lies in favour of inventor-type researchers: but we have little knowledge of how to identify them; train them; utilize them. All we can know is that there seem few of them in educational research. If we knew something about social science researchers generally perhaps the pool of workers available for education would be increased. Education could be a field of great adventure to some—but it frequently remains unvisited because of non-awareness, prejudice, and the University tradition of separate departments.

To conclude, then, the characteristics, values, motives, and creativity of researchers (albeit scientists and inventors) are different from other groups in society, but are united by values which rate theoretical and aesthetic interests and problems higher than economic, social, or other values. It seems that the working of an R & D market would be hampered by such views: that the supply of research workers would not readily adjust to the changing direction of sponsors' requirements.

Uncertainty and the production relations for knowledge and information

The other major assumption in research policy making is that by investing heavily in certain areas, there will be an increase in knowledge/inventions in that area. Economists usually call the input—output relation a production function: a description of the relations between the input components and the derived output which allows some analysis of production and cost relationships. It is probable that R & D has very different production relations from most other commodities. The production of knowledge is characterized by very high levels of uncertainty; by a poor market for appropriating the results of productive effort; by public control over the production resources and most of the mechanisms for purchasing and using the outcomes.

The production of knowledge is characterized by uncertainty. Indeed it is one of the paradoxes of the economics of R & D that 'the product of the research and development effort is an observation on the world which reduces its possible range of variation . . . (and) it is intimately connected with the problem of uncertainty reduction . . . (Arrow 1969) and yet at the same time the production process of R & D itself . . . 'is an activity often carried on under conditions of great uncertainty' (Nelson 1959b). The interest shown by economists stems from the importance of technology in generating economic growth and the recognition that R & D and Education and 'advances in knowledge' represent a significant part of the unexplained residual in growth accounting (Denison 1964; Robinson and Vaizey (Eds), 1966). This major interest has as usual yielded further difficulties which have generated much literature but which must be left out of the discussion (Blaug, 1970; Nordhaus, 1969); see also the review article on Technical Progress which has a section on R & D (Kennedy & Thirlwall, 1972).

Given the uncertainty, it is difficult to see how a policy could be formulated which had conviction. On the one hand, sponsors seem to claim that they can identify the problem areas and on the other hand units are established staffed by those who perhaps do not hold the view that such problems can be solved in the time and with the resources available. If problem solving is correlated with interest and interest with skills then the performer is perhaps the individual best able to reveal both the area to be researched and the methods, resources and time-span needed to achieve some kind of success.

Many problems of course are not uncertain. Most development projects in educational research for example have tangible products and at least the presumption that the new methods/material are better than alternatives. The Schools Council therefore has a somewhat easier task than, say, SSRC where 'success' is difficult to recognize and a product or outcome is so intangible. However, if the Rothschild criteria of a 90 per cent probability of success is applied to development projects, then there would certainly be problems even for the Schools Council.

The point to be made, then, is that production relations in R & D are uncertain. Increasing inputs may not lead to increased output at any given time or for any given project: although it is probable that a general increase in R & D allocation would see a general increase in outcomes.

A related difficulty is the objectives of sponsors. These are so little understood that any discussion of their effects on the forming of research policy would be premature. It is remarkable that we have so little information about Foundations, because, as Chapter 3 has revealed, they are important elements in the funding of social science R & D. The objectives, however, remain unknown, although one may make research speculations as Tullock (1966) and Newhouse (1970) have done in their suggestive work on the theory of non-profit institutions.

The main point of this work—and of much of the earlier discussion in Chapter 3—is that there are few external incentives to efficiency or productivity in such institutions. As Tullock points out, there is an irreconcilable conflict of resource allocation: publicity and information flows can only be purchased at the expense of a reduction in activities which reflect the main objectives of the Foundations. Newhouse points to the maximand of such institutions as being prestige and respectability which probably is best achieved by high quality services and other work. His examples are taken from hospitals but there is a close parallel in the work of the Trusts and Foundations.

Other sponsors of educational R & D such as SSRC, DES, and Schools Council have different objectives both from each other and from the private Trusts and Foundations. Some discussion was offered in Chapter 3 about their activities and the point to be made here is that the maximizing or optimizing or even 'satisficing' (Simon, 1959) of their objectives is not easy in a conceptual sense and seems most complex in any practical or empirical sense of measuring success or achievement. If the allocation of funds within educational R & D is to be rational and systematic it seems essential that the objectives of performers, sponsors and users be optimized: yet there seems to be no reason to suppose that the present arrangements permit such a mutual reconciliation of all three interests.

The conclusion of this section is that a formulation of policy seems to imply greater faith in market responses than is at present justified. The production of knowledge may not respond to direction of resources by sponsors because the supply side—the performer—is only partially motivated by resource acquisition; and the 'success' of R & D is so uncertain that it is at least probable that the performer is best able to select projects which engage his interest and hence are likely to succeed. If sponsors' requirements (and directions) coincide with performers' interests then the market should operate smoothly. If conflicts occur then resources are likely to be misallocated. Sponsors' criteria could eventually lead to an unbalanced research effort: the usual problem of too much development work, policy oriented, or conclusion-oriented work and too little basic research. This has been stressed sufficiently already.

A more serious matter is that in-house research, and the close-circuiting of the performer—sponsor network may misallocate the supply of funds. Once committed to the support of such research units and in-house research work it is difficult to imagine that sponsors will abandon them. The net quantity of research funds available to the rest of the research community is thereby diminished. It is not suggested that the total funds are likely to be affected by such policies —merely that the net disposable funds will be diminished because certain funds are reserved by the sponsors for their own use. This may be efficient research administration: but the production of knowledge seems at present to be very closely geared to the sponsors' notion of what is needed. Perhaps it is natural that the market should change like this but the full implications of such policy (and institutional) changes need to be closely monitored and deserve a full analysis.

The utilization of research outcomes

If knowledge is characterized by uncertainty in its production relations then sponsors will wish to be convinced that past results are utilized. Research outputs rely for their effective use on transmission mechanisms to ensure that the three or four objectives of educational R & D are satisfied. Hence the important relationship between utilization and information channels.

It is a source of perennial comment that the dissemination of research-based information throughout the educational system is poor. There are a number of recent developments—the NFER's popular series of research reports; the willingness of the Schools Council to extend the life of some projects to allow and encourage the results to diffuse through the system; and the short notices attached to most of the SSRC projects. Nevertheless, 'these do not add up to a coherent system of information and dissemination. There are still huge gaps, not only in the teacher's knowledge of research findings that might be useful to him, but also in the means that researchers have available for finding out about what is going on elsewhere in their own field of interest. Any hopeful prospect for educational research requires that information, dissemination and abstracting services be still further improved' (Taylor, 1972).

The use of information in policy making and the information needs of educational administrators in an area of the educational system about which very little is known. Educational administration as a subject for study is of relatively recent origins (see Baron and Taylor, 1969) and a systematic examination of information requirements for educational administration has yet to be undertaken. There is of course some uneasiness between research workers and policy makers. On the one hand it is probably the case that most decisions and policies are made without any direct use of information either because none is available, or if it can be used it requires modification or interpretation. It is of course rare for research to be applied directly. On the other hand researchers prefer broader problems than the relatively narrow action or policy-oriented research which can arise from a very close association of research and policy making, and they are also a little suspicious and sceptical of the interpretation and use of many research results (see Husén and Boalt, 1967). This unfortunate climate of opinion which exists between administration and research derives as usual from a misunderstanding of the purposes and methods of the two activities. Administrators often fail to realize the limitations of a particular piece of research and the potential value of a body of related research or a particular topic. It is doubtful if a single piece of work—except the large-scale longitudinal studies—can greatly assist decisions. Reviews of 'new' knowledge based on several pieces of related research work however are often very helpful if used carefully. Researchers for their part often underestimate the financial and political constraints under which administrators work—it is not simply a matter of forming policy and making decisions—it is a matter of knowing what is possible and obtaining consent to policies. It is also a matter of operating within very narrow limits for change. Education rarely changes dramatically—and research results where used can point to directions for change and prepare the way for gradual piecemeal innovation (see Stufflebeam *et al.*, 1971; Yates, 1971). The whole area of educational change, policy formulation, and information inputs to the decision-making process based on R & D results makes a fascinating but complex study. It is not possible to cover the ground here because the range of literature is so diverse as to make the topic a major digression. However, it seems useful to point to what might be done. Braybrooke and Lindblom's (1963) major work must be mentioned as the starting point of any study of the policy making process, Castle, Murray and Potter (1971), and the Open University course unit on decision-making (1971) open up some interesting lines of approach. The difficulty lies in relating decisions to information requirements and the information channels available. There is very little work available which indicates how information is selected, channelled, and used, nor is there on going work which relates information theory to decision theory despite the close relations of the two disciplines. There is also the crucial economic aspects of information. Clearly, there are variations in costs involved in acquiring information and hence some means of assigning a 'value' to information is needed. The literature here is in its infancy (see Marshak, 1968; Arrow, 1971). Another economic aspect of information is the cost of *producing* the information, i.e. the R & D work which provides the knowledge base for information flows. R & D has yet to be successfully integrated with information theory, decision theory and the innovation/utilization literature in a coherent theory of knowledge and information. It is enough that the point has been made—the main topic here must be educational R & D and educational change.

Educational R & D usually acts slowly on the climate of opinion. It indicates the areas of change, the areas of importance, the areas of concern. It points up the successful and the difficult activities which exist within the system and, insofar as such findings are relevant, it guides decision making. Even if such results are not cited during the decision making process, it is likely that a well informed administrator will consider the main elements of the findings even if he cannot place the exact details of the work. As Taylor (1972) has pointed out 'for the most part the influence of research has been to sensitize'.

The process of innovation

If one can combine the three different purposes of educational research into a single objective then it is likely that that objective would be to relate R & D to educational innovation. Innovation includes aspects of all the objectives—it involves policies and decision making; it is usually carried out by teachers and schools; it is sometimes affected by public/social opinion; and it is either instigated by or stimulates new parallel advances in knowledge.

We know very little about the innovation process even at the theoretical level, although the early work of Mort (1946; Mort and Connell, 1941) and the collection of basic studies by Miles (1964) are useful. There are alternative models of the process but none has been developed to a point where it is possible to test it. The usual model is the linear model tacitly assumed by Guba (1967a, 1967b) Clark and Guba (1966; 1967; see also discussion in Yates, 1971). This argues that research leads to development possibilities which are undertaken and which then lead to the adoption of innovations. There is thus a series of definable (albeit not distinctive) steps from basic research through invention, design, development, installation and adoption of innovations. Each step is fairly self contained in that different institutions perform the different tasks suggested by each of separate steps. It is a model that has a tidy, institutionalized appeal and of course one can find some evidence from the natural sciences and education that the model approximates to the real world.

Another model stresses the discontinuities which exist between the various steps. The decision making process is very different in the research from the adoption/installation stage; the rules of evidence, the constraints operating on the process are very different at the dissemination stage and the invention stage of the process. Thus, this model (Gideonse, 1968) tends to treat the innovation process as a discrete series of connected steps rather than a related continuum with characteristics peculiar to each part of the process. Gideonse identifies three parts: research, development and school-based operations and shows how each are independent with different criteria governing their behaviour. Although related, the research and development functions have many discontinuities.

The 'linkage' model can be identified by several papers mostly by administrators. Here the three functions of research, development and dissemination are acknowledged but there is an insistence on the need for a close linking between research and development. It is seen for example in the USOE staff—(see Mason and Boyah, 1968) and among some educational researchers who wish for a greater involvement between researchers and those who actually innovate. Glaser (1968) and Wittlock and Wiley (1970) for example argue that innovation is not an automatic outcome of research: that without much closer linkages the institutional and intellectual barriers between researchers and practitioners are too strong to allow a 'natural' linear relationship to prosper.

The role of dissemination in providing these linkages is fairly obvious in principle, but rather complex in practice. Information of itself is no great incentive to change—and the reluctance to read let alone act on research results has been noted. The general work on innovation stresses the importance of individual contact (Carlson, 1965; Rogers, 1962; Rogers and Shoemaker, 1971; Havelock, 1969, 1971) in the diffusion of invention and best practice. To use British examples (Burns and Stalker, 1966; Carter and Williams, 1957), it also appears necessary to have sympathetic management who are willing and able to adopt new techniques/products as these become available through the innovation process. Industrial and commercial case studies are perhaps not too appropriate for a study of educational change. The contrast between the adoption of new processes in industry (Carter and Williams, 1958) and the adoption of educational reorganization in Sweden (Husén and Boalt, 1967) and in an LEA (Frith, 1963; Saran, 1967) reveals, as one would expect, as many differences as similarities. Besides, the range of cases available is too small to make many certain statements—except the perennial but justifiable plea for more research. Until we develop some closer understanding of the innovation process much of the current concern over the value/rationale for educational research must remain unanswered. Research is needed: innovation is essential.

The dangers of misuse or misunderstanding of research are usually less serious than simply ignoring a body of work. Nevertheless, Wall and Husén, (1968) have made the appropriate comments on the suitable relationship between research and policy making: the freedom and independence of the researcher should be safeguarded, yet the information should be useable by the policy makers in any way they wish. It is not at all unusual for policy decisions to be made in advance of research work—which, if commissioned, is then likely to be used to justify the decision or used selectively to rationalize the current situation. It is this kind of use which researchers distrust and even in Sweden, which is taken to be the model of research-based decision making, it is argued that although 'the establishment of nation-wide machinery for the forming and implementation of educational policy would not suffice unless the machinery included bodies for research and planning' . . . (and) . . .

'to safeguard against corruption the researchers should be independent of politicians . . .' (Husén and Boalt, 1968). In the UK relationships between the research community and administrators and policymakers are too distant for such problems to be pressing. If future decisions and policies are to have a firmer knowledge base then perhaps this Swedish experience will prove valuable.

Conclusions

It has been shown that about £2m p.a. of externally funded research work was undertaken during the years 1968 to 1970, together with a further £0·5m of university research work. This total represents 0·13 per cent of total educational expenditure. There is no theoretical or empirical rationale for deciding on the appropriate level of expenditure—but the arguments of Wall and Chase that more is needed are very persuasive. It is almost beyond doubt that we know so little about the educational system and the various educational processes involved that more money and manpower 'should be' devoted to searching for difficulties and understanding. As Chase argued, our knowledge base is so weak that it must be possible to allocate and utilize our current £2400m expenditure more effectively if only we can produce and disseminate information efficiently. In short, we need greater resources for educational research.

It is not enough to demand more—the market arrangements within which knowledge is produced and transmitted also need strengthening. It is, however, a rather delicate balance of the possible and the desirable. On the one hand there is every need to maintain a pluralist position among sponsors—it would be most undesirable for a single body or group to have sole power over the allocation of funds. On the other hand, there is the need for greater coordination of priorities and more information as to the criteria or policies of sponsors. Such information would be in everybody's interest—it forces sponsors to provide a rationale for decisions and non-decisions and it avoids wasted time and resources by those performers who seek funds. Few things are more frustrating to performers than the rejection of applications for reasons which, if known in advance, could easily have been avoided. The point, then, is to achieve greater coordination, better information flows and improve the rationale and the consistency of decision making among sponsors without reducing their numbers or independence.

Performers, too, need to be strengthened. Much of the research effort is scattered and fragmented and it is noticeable that only a dozen or so universities can mount a serious research effort. The enormous importance of the large, well-established departments at London, Manchester, Bristol and elsewhere is too marked not to be significant. The Massey Report (Great Britain, Council for Scientific Policy, 1971) also noticed this point and argued that a minimum level of domestic research was necessary before external contract work could be successfully undertaken. Few Education departments could meet the tests (see Taylor, 1972 for brief discussion).

The performer—sponsor relationship in the research market is complicated by the problem of uncertainty. This sets a constraint on the production of knowledge which may affect decision making by sponsors because of the capacity of the performer to undertake work dominated by policy considerations where deadlines may be important. In the more important and more general case, setting priorities and increasing resources in a given area may not yield results because the production of knowledge is characterized by the level of uncertainty, although development work is of course much more certain in its outcomes. It is also peculiar to the extent that performers are motivated by non-economic objectives. Unless performers' interests are engaged in the topic selected by sponsors there is no reason to suppose that the best research staff are attached to the subject or that new knowledge of appropriate quantity and quality will emerge.

A delicate balance is also necessary between the types and the methods of educational research. There has been a fairly strong line of argument that more basic research is needed: that the knowledge base, on which most of the development work, the mission and policy or decision orientated work is funded, is very weak. The figures in Chapter 2 are rather misleading because it is relatively easy to define development and hence the 'hard' figure is the development figure. The residual figure is basic research—although many projects which on closer scrutiny can hardly be called basic research have to fall into this category. Difficult though it is to justify, there is a need for more basic work in education.

The methods used raise other issues. It will be remembered that Lazarfeld and Sieber (1964), supported by much British evidence—the Massey Report, the evidence of the large University Education Departments and the SSRC Research Units—argued that size, autonomy and full time 'bureau' based research was more productive and satisfactory than the traditional individual scholarship work. This seems undeniable for the large scale, statistically based survey and experimental work such as the Plowden research studies, and longitudinal studies such as the Primary French project and the Comprehensive project at NFER. Most development studies also fall into this category. There is, however, a need for small scale, experimental, innovative work. Ideally, as Young (1965) suggested there should be some experimental schools or perhaps classes where new ideas and methods could be carried out and evaluated. Case studies are a valuable research tool if they suggest more general hypotheses which can be tested on a wider scale. It is also the case that understanding may be facilitated by close observation and interviews in a way not possible in the large-scale statistical exercises. It is clear that both methods are needed: it is the role of the professional researcher to select those instruments and methods that can analyse most carefully and accurately the problem to be solved. It is simply that the balance of methodology is important if refinement of the instruments is to be achieved. Both methods are probably best accomplished in large, self-contained units, institutes, bureaux or other 'independent' places.

Another type of research which is much neglected—indeed Comprehensive Education and the French Project are the only two examples available—is the evaluation or monitoring of policy decisions. It is often the case that decisions have to be taken *before* evidence of consequences is available. It is obvious that the effects of teaching French in the primary school cannot be known until large numbers of children are actually taught the language. The crucial point however is that decisions of this kind should have an automatic evaluation unit appointed at the start of the policy implementation. In this way there is every chance that educational change can be understood and improved and revised decisions can be made if necessary. Evaluation raises all the matters discussed earlier including the 'no significant difference' problem, but it seems the only method available with which to measure and assess the effects of innovation and policy decisions. It will be interesting to see some of the studies on the raising of the school leaving age.

Finally, there is the point that the research—development—innovation—adoption—decision making process is not well understood. It is one of the prime arguments in any discussion of the rationale for educational R & D and one of the least understood. It involves the dissemination process, the role and attitudes of the practitioners, the decision making process particularly at school and LEA levels, and the evaluation of educational change. Some case studies of innovation are badly needed and it may be that this indirect approach would allow a closer understanding of R & D-Innovation models.

It remains but to repeat that educational R & D has at least three objectives—advances in knowledge, improvement in practice and aids to decision making. The resources for educational R & D need to be increased and the research market needs to be strengthened if educational R & D is to be a powerful aid to the understanding and promotion of innovations and educational change in the next decade.

APPENDIX 1

Performers: Independent Institutions

Associated Lancashire Schools Examining Board, Manchester
Association for the Study of Medical Education
Association of Teachers of Russian

British Association
British Association of the Hard of Hearing
British Medical Association
British National Bibliography

Cambridge Education Committee
Catholic Blind Institute
Centre for Information on Language Teaching
Clifton College and Marlborough College
Committee of Vice-Chancellors and Principals
Commonwealth Society for the Deaf

Development Group of Architects and Building Branch

East Midland Regional Examinations Board
Engineering Design Consultants

Furniture Industry Research Association
Further Education Staff College, Blagdon, Bristol

General Register Office
Glamorgan Education Committee

Independent Assessment and Research Centre
Institut des Sciences de l'Education, Geneva
International Association for the Evaluation of Educational Achievement
International Baccalaureate Office, London

Local Government Operational Research Unit
London Borough of Havering

Metropolitan Regional Examinations Board, London
Middlesex Hospital
Moor House Special School

National Children's Bureau
National Council for Educational Technology
National Examinations Board in Supervisory Studies
National Foundation for Educational Research
National Industrial Fuel Efficiency Service
National Institute of Adult Education
National Society for Mentally Handicapped Children
Nuffield Foundation

Parliamentary Group for World Government
Political and Economic Planning

Royal College of Art

Schools Council
Society for Research into Higher Education
South Western Examinations Board
Southern Film Productions, Brockenhurst
Southern Regional Council for Further Education
Southern Regional Examinations Board
Dr J. E. Spice (private individual)
Stoke Mandeville Hospital Trust
Student Christian Movement/University Teachers' Group
System Research Limited

Tavistock Institute
Thurrock Technical College, Essex
Towyn School, Merioneth

Universities Council for the Education of Teachers

West Midlands Examination Board
West Riding Social Education Centre

Young Women's Christian Association

APPENDIX 2

Sources of Funds for Educational Research and Development

Baxi Trust
Bernard Van Leer Foundation

Carnegie Foundation for the Advancement of Teaching

Department of Education and Science

Educational Foundation for Visual Aids

Ford Foundation

Gulbenkian Foundation

Home Office

Leverhulme Trust Fund

National Children's Bureau
National Council for Educational Technology
National Foundation for Educational Research
Nuffield Foundation

Office for Scientific and Technical Information

Rockefeller Foundation, New York
Rowntree Charitable Trust
Rowntree Memorial Trust

Schools Council
Social Science Research Council
Society for Mentally Handicapped Children

Wolfson Foundation

REFERENCES

ALLISON, D. (Ed.) (1969). *The R & D Game*. Cambridge, Mass.: MIT Press.

ARROW, K. (1962). 'Economic welfare and the allocation of resources for invention' in NELSON, R. R. (Ed.), *The Rate and Direction of Inventive Activity*. NBER Special Conference Series No. 13, New Jersey: Princeton University Press.

ARROW, K. J. (1969). 'Classificatory notes on the production and transmission of technological knowledge', *Amer. Econ. Rev.*, May, 29–35.

ARROW, K. J. (1971). 'The value of and demand for information'. Reprinted in *Essays in Theory and Risk-Bearing*. Chicago: Markham.

ASHBY, SIR E. (1963). 'Introduction: decision-making in the academic world', *Sociological Studies in British Universities, Educational Monograph No. 7*, The Sociological Review, Keele University, p. 6. Also quoted in BLAUG, M. (Ed.) (1969), *Economics of Education 2*. Harmondsworth: Penguin, p. 320.

BARON, G., and TAYLOR, W. (1969). *Educational Administration and the Social Sciences*. University of London: Athlone Press.

BLAUG, M. (Ed.) (1969). *Economics of Education 2*. Harmondsworth: Penguin.

BLAUG, M. (1970). *An Introduction to the Economics of Education*. London: Allen Lane, The Penguin Press.

BLOOM, B. (1968). 'R & D centers: promise and fulfilment', *J. Res. & Devel. in Educ.*, **1**, 4, 181–9.

BOYAN, N. J. (1969). 'The political realities of education R & D', *J. Res. & Eval. in Educ.*, **2**, 4, 3–18. Harmondsworth: Penguin.

BOYLE, E., and CROSSLAND, A. (1971). *The Politics of Education*. Harmondsworth: Penguin.

BRAYBROOKE, D., and LINDLOM, C. E. (1963). *A Strategy of Decision*. New York: Free Press.

BROSAN, G., CARTER, C., LAYARD, P. R. G., VENABLES, P., and WILLIAMS, G. (1970). *Patterns and Policies on Higher Education*. Harmondsworth: Penguin.

BURNS, T., and STALKER, G. W. (1966). *The Management of Innovation*. London: Tavistock Publications.

BUTCHER, H. J. (1968). *Educational Research in Britain*. London: University of London Press.

BYATT, I. C. R., and COHEN, A. V. (1969). 'An attempt to quantify the economic benefits of scientific research', *Science Policy Studies No. 4*. London: HMSO, DES.

CANE, B., and SCHROEDER, C. (1971). *The Teacher and Research*. Slough: NFER.

CARLSON, R. (1965). *The Adoption of Educational Innovations*. Center for the Advance Study of Educational Administration: Oregon University Press.

CARTER, C., and WILLIAMS, B. (1957). *Industry and Technical Progress*. London: Oxford University Press.

CARTER, C., and WILLIAMS, B. (1958). *Investment in Innovation*. London: Oxford University Press.

CASTLES, F. G., MURRAY, D. J., and POTTER, D. C. (1971). *Decisions, Organizations and Society*. Harmondsworth: Penguin Books for the Open University.

CENTRAL ADVISORY COUNCIL FOR EDUCATION (ENGLAND) (1967). *Children and their Primary Schools*. London: HMSO. (Plowden Report.)

CENTRAL ADVISORY COUNCIL FOR EDUCATION (ENGLAND) (1959 and 1960). *15 to 18*. Vol. 1: *Report* 1959, Vol. 2: *Survey* 1960. London: HMSO. (Crowther Report.)

CHASE, F. S. (1968). 'Educational R & D: promise or mirage', *J. Res. and Develop. in Educ.*, **1**, 4, 3–24.

CHASE, F. S. (1969). 'The R & D institutional base: what more is needed?', *J. Res. and Devel. in Educ.*, **2**, 4, 19–28.

CHASE, F. S. (1970). 'The laboratories 1970 and beyond', *J. Res. and Devel. in Educ.*, **3**, 2, 104–20.

CLARK, D. L., and GUBA, E. G. (1966). 'Effecting change in institutions of higher education'. UNESCO Institute of Education, Mimeo.

CLARK, D. L., and GUBA, E. G. (1967). 'An examination of potential change roles in education', in SAND, O. (Ed.), *Rational Planning in Curricula and Instruction*. Washington, D.C.: NEA, 111–34.

COLE, H., and VAN DE EYKEN, W. (1971). *Survey of Current Research in Further Education*. London: Hutchinson Educational.

COMMITTEE OF VICE-CHANCELLORS AND PRINCIPALS OF THE UNIVERSITIES OF THE UNITED KINGDOM (1972). *Report of an Inquiry into the Use of Academic Staff Time*. London: CVC.

COUNCIL OF EUROPE (1970 and 1971). *Educational Research: European Survey*. 2 Vols. Strasbourg.

CRONBACH, L. J., and SUPPES, P. (Eds.) (1969). *Research for Tomorrow's Schools*. London: Macmillan.

DAVIS, R. H. (1971). 'Institutional accountability: all, some or none', *J. Res. and Devel. in Educ.*, **5**, 1, 26–31.

DENISON, E. (1964). 'Measuring the contribution of education (and the residual) to economic growth', in VAIZEY, J. (Ed.), *The Residual Factor and Economic Growth*. Paris: OECD.

DROR, Y., and PLOWMAN, D. E. G. (1970). 'Two comments on Dr Riecken's Article', *Soc. Sc. Inf.*, **9**, 1, 187–96.

Educational Researcher, 1970, December.

EDUCATIONAL TESTING SERVICE (1971). 'Proceedings of the conference on educational accountability', Mimeo, Princeton, N.J., USA.

EDWARDS, R. (1968). 'Educational research and the training of researchers in Canada', *Canadian Educational and Research Digest*, **8**, 4, December.

ERAULT, M., and SQUIRES, G. (1971). *An Amended Select Bibliography of Educational Technology*. London: NCET.

FIRTH, G. C. (1963). 'Comprehensive schools in Coventry and elsewhere', City of Coventry Education Committee.

GIDEONSE, H. (1968). 'Research development, and the improvement of education', *Science*, **162**, Nov. 1.

GLASER, R. (1970). 'Evaluation of instruction and changing educational models', in WITTROCK, M. C. and WILEY, D. E. (Eds.) *Evaluation of Instruction.* New York: Holt Reinhart and Winston.

GREAT BRITAIN. CIVIL SERVICE, 1968. *The Civil Service: Report of the Committee, 1966–8*, Vol. 1. London: HMSO.

GREAT BRITAIN. COUNCIL FOR SCIENTIFIC POLICY, 1968. *Inquiry into the Flow of Candidates in Science and Technology.* London: HMSO. (Dainton Report.)

GREAT BRITAIN. COUNCIL FOR SCIENTIFIC POLICY, 1971. *Report of a Study on the Support of Scientific Research in the Universities.* London: HMSO. (Massey Report.)

GREAT BRITAIN. DEPARTMENT OF EDUCATION AND SCIENCE, 1963. *Report on Higher Education.* London: HMSO. (Robbins Reports.)

GREAT BRITAIN. DEPARTMENT OF EDUCATION AND SCIENCE. *Statistics of Education*, Vol. 3, 1969; Vol. 4, 1970; Vol. 5, 1971; Vol. 6, 1972. London: HMSO.

GREAT BRITAIN. DEPARTMENT OF EDUCATION AND SCIENCE, 1970. *Output Budgeting for the DES.* London: HMSO.

GREAT BRITAIN. DEPARTMENT OF EDUCATION AND SCIENCE AND MINISTRY OF TECHNOLOGY, 1971. *Statistics of Science and Technology*, 1970. London: HMSO.

GREAT BRITAIN, 1971. *A Framework for Government Research and Development*, Cmnd. 4814. London: HMSO. (The Rothschild Report.)

GRILICHES, Z. (1958). 'Research costs and social returns: hybrid corn and related innovations', *J. Pol. Econ.*, **66**, October, 419–31.

GRILICHES, Z. (1964). 'Research expenditures, education and the aggregate agricultural production function', *Amer. Econ. Rev.*, **54**, December, 118–30.

GUBA, E. G. (1967a). 'Methodological strategies for educational research'. Paper presented at UNESCO Institute for Education Conference, Mimeo.

GUBA, E. G. (1967b). 'The basis for educational improvement'. UNESCO Institute for Education, Mimeo.

GUBA, E. G. (1969). 'Significant differences', *Educational Researcher*, **XX**, 3, AERA Newsletter.

HART, D. (1972). *Daily Telegraph Suppl.*, April 7th.

HARTLEY, H. J. (1968). *Educational Planning—Programming Budgeting.* New York: Prentice Hall.

HAVELOCK, R. G. (1971). 'The utilization of educational research and development', *Brit. J. Educ. Tech.*, **2**, 2, 84–98.

HAVELOCK, R., *et al.* (1969). 'Planning for innovation through dissemination and utilization of knowledge'. Institute for Social Research, University of Michigan.

HAYMAN, J. L. (1968). *Research in Education.* Columbia, Ohio: Charles E. Merrill, Pub. Co.

HIGGINS, G. W., and JESSOP, W. N. (1965). *Communication in the Building Industry.* London: Tavistock Publications.

HIRSCHMAN, A. O., and LINDBLOM, C. E. (1962). 'Economic development, research and development, policy making: some convergent views', *Beh. Sc.*, **7**, 211–22.

HUSEN, T., and BOALT, G. (1968). *Educational Research and Educational Change.* New York: Wiley.

JENKINS, W. I., and VELODY, I. (1970). 'The social sciences and government: do the natural sciences show the prescribed path?', *Soc. Sc. Inf.*, **9**, 5, 91–118.

JEWKES, J., SAWERS, D., and STILLERMAN, R. (1969) (2nd ed.). *The Source of Invention.* London: Macmillan.

KENNEDY, C., and THIRLWALL, A. P. (1972). 'Surveys in applied economics: technical progress', *Econ. J.*, March, 11–67.

KLEIN, B., and MECKLING, W. (1958). 'Application of operation research to development decisions', *Operation Research,* **6**, 352–63.

LAZARFELD, P., and SIEBER, S. (1964). *Organizing Educational Research.* New York: Prentice Hall.

LINDBLOM, C. (1968). *The Policy Making Process.* New York: Prentice Hall.

MADDOX, J. (1964). 'Choice and the scientific community', *Minerva*, **2**, 141.

MANSFIELD, E. (1969). *Economics of Technological Change.* London: Longmans.

MARGOLIS, J., and GUITTON, H. (Eds.) (1970). *Public Economics.* London: Macmillan.

MARSCHAK, J. (1968). 'Economics of inquiring, communicating, deciding', *Am. Econ. Rev.*, **58**, 2, 1–18.

MASON, W. S., and BOYAN, N. J. (1968). 'Perspectives on R & D Centers', *J. of R & D in Educ.*, **1**, 4, 190–202.

MCKINNON, D. (1962). 'Intellect and motive in scientific inventions: implication for supply', in NELSON, R. R. (Ed.) *The Rate and Direction of Inventive Activity.* NBER Special Conference Series No. 13. New Jersey: Princeton University Press, 361–84.

MILES, M. B. (Ed.) (1964). *Innovation in Education.* Columbia: Teacher's College Press.

MORT, P. R. (1946). *Principles of School Administration.* New York: McGraw Hill.

MORT, P. R., and CONNELL, F. G. (1941). *American School in Transition.* Columbia: Teacher's College Press.

NELSON, R. R. (1959a). 'The economics of invention: a survey of the literature', *J. of Business.* Chicago University, April, 101–27.

NELSON, R. R. (1959b). 'The simple economics of basic scientific research', *J. Pol. Econy.*, **4**, 269–90.

NEWHOUSE, S. P. (1970). 'Towards an economic theory of non-profit institutions: an economic model of a hospital', *Am. Econ. Rev.*, **60**, 64–74.
'The Rothschild row examined', in *New Society*, 13.1.72, 70–2.

NEW SOCIETY (1972b). 'Social science and the Rothschild report' (The SSRC Statement), 17.2.72, 341–4.

NORDHAUS, W. D. (1969). *Invention, Growth and Welfare.* Camb. Mass. USA: MIT Press.

NUFFIELD FOUNDATION (1966/7, 1968/9). Annual Reports.

OECD (1969). 'Educational R & D in the US; Examiners Report. Paris: Restricted circulation.

OECD (1970). *Educational Policies for the 1970s.* Paris: OECD.

OECD (1971). *Educational R & D in the US.* Paris: OECD.

ORLANS, H. (1968). 'Making social research more useful to government', *Soc. Sc. Inf.*, **7**, 6, 151–8.

PESTON, M. (1969). 'Economics and administration of education' in BARON, G. and TAYLOR, W. *Educational Administration and the Social Sciences*. University of London: Athlone Press.

PIDGEON, D. A. (1971). 'The work of the NFER'. Address to the AGM and Conference of the NFER, December. Unpublished.

POLANYI, M. (1962). 'The republic of science: its political and economic theory', *Minerva*, **1**, 1, Autumn.

POPPER, Sir K. (1957). *The Poverty of Historicism*. London: Routledge & Kegan Paul.

RADFORD, W. C. (1967). 'Research into education'. ACER Conference, Mimeo.

RAISBECK, G., *et al.* (1965). *Management Factors Affecting Research and Exploratory Development*. Boston, Mass.: Arthur D. Little Inc.

REAGAN, M. D. (1967). 'Basic and applied research: a meaningful distinction?', *Science*, **155**, 1383–6.

RIECKEN, H. W. (1969). 'Social science and social problems', *Soc. Sc. Inf.*, **8**, 1, 101–29.

ROBINSON, E. (1968). *The New Polytechnics*. London: Cornmarket Press.

ROBINSON, E. A. G., and VAIZEY, J. *The Economics of Education*. London: Macmillan.

ROGERS, E. M. (1962). *The Diffusion of Innovations*. New York: Free Press.

ROGERS, E. M., and SHOEMAKER, F. (1971) (2nd ed.). *Communications of Innovations: a cross-cultural approach*. New York: Free Press.

ROSE, H., and ROSE, S. (1970). *Science and Society*. Harmondsworth: Penguin.

ROSSMAN, M. J. (1931). *The Psychology of the Inventor*. New Hampshire, Washington: Inventors Pub. Co.

SARAN, R. (1967). 'Decision-making by a local education authority', *Public Administration*, Winter, 387–402.

SCHOOLS COUNCIL (1968/9, 1969/70). Annual Reports. London: Evans/Methuen.

SIMON, H. A. (1959). 'Theory of decision-making in economics and behavioural science, *Am. Econ. Rev.*, **49**, 253–83.

SPAGHT, S. 'Accountability through performance continuity', *Acc. J. of Res & Dev. in Educ.*, **5**, 1, 71–8.

SSRC (1970) (1971, 1972). Annual Reports 1968/9, 1969/70, 1970/1. London: HMSO.

STOKE ON TRENT (1963). Education Committee, *Am. J.*

STORER, N. W. (1966). *The Social System of Science*. New York: Holt, Rinehart & Winston.

STUFFLEBEAM, D. (Ed.) (1971). *Educational Evaluation and Decision Making*. Illinois, USA: Peacock Publs.

TAYLOR, C. W., and BARRON, F. (1963). *Scientific Creativity*. New York: Wiley.

TAYLOR, W. (1965). Appendix, in: YOUNG, M. (ed.), *Innovation and Research in Education*. London: Routledge & Kegan Paul.

TAYLOR, W. (1970). *Policy and Planning for Post-Secondary Education—A European Overview*. Strasbourg: Council for Europe.

TAYLOR, W. (1972). 'Retrospect and prospect in educational research'. Paper to the NFER AGM 1971, *Educ. Res.*, **15**, 1, 3–9.

THATCHER, M. (1970). Address to the Annual Conference of NFER. December. Unpublished.

TIBBLE, J. W. (Ed.) (1966). *The Study of Education.* London: Routledge & Kegan Paul.

TOULMIN, S. (1958). *The Philosophy of Science.* London: Hutchinson.

TOULMIN, S. 'The complexity of scientific choice', *Minerva,* **II**, 141.

TRAVERS, R. M. W. (1964) (2nd ed.). *An Introduction to Educational Research.* London: Macmillan.

TULLOCK, G. (1966). 'Information without profit', in TULLOCK, G. (Ed.) *Papers on Non-market Decision Making.* University of Virginia, 141–59. Reprinted in LAMBERTON, D. M. (Ed.) (1971). *Economics of Information and Knowledge,* 119–30. Harmondsworth: Penguin.

WALL, W. D. (1959). 'Educational research and the needs of the schools'. Address to Nat. Assoc. of Inspectors of Schools and Educational Organizers.

WALL, W. D. (1962). 'Resistances, organization and costs', *Br. J. Educ. Psychol.,* Nov., 224–33.

WALL, W. D. (1968). 'The work of the NFER', in BUTCHER, H. J. (Ed.) *Educational Research in Britain.* London: Hutchinson.

WALL, W. D., and HUSEN, T. (1968). *Educational Research and Policy Making.* Slough: NFER.

WALSH, W. H. (1953). *The Philosophy of History.* London: Hutchinson.

WEINBERG, A. M. (1963, 1964). 'Criteria for scientific choice', *Minerva,* **1**, 59, and **III**, 3.

WISEMAN, S. (1962). 'The tools of research—man and machines', *Br. J. Educ. Psychol.,* Nov., 218–23.

WISEMAN, S. (1970). Preface to CANE, B., and SCHROEDER, C. *The Teacher and Research.* Slough: NFER.

WISEMAN, S. (1973). 'The educational obstacle race: factors that hinder pupil progress'. Paper to NFER AGM, Dec. 1970, *Educ. Res.,* **15**, 2, 87–93.

WISEMAN, S., and PIDGEON, D. A. (1970). *Curriculum Evaluation.* Slough: NFER.

WITTROCK, M. C., and WILEY, D. E. (Eds.) (1970). *Evaluation of Instruction.* New York: Holt, Rinehart and Winston.

WRIGLEY, J. (1970). 'The work of the Schools Council', in BUTCHER, H. J., and PONT, H. B. (Eds.) *Educational Research in Britain, Vol. 2.* London: University of London Press.

YATES, A. (Ed.) (1971). *The Role of Research in Educational Change.* UNESCO Institute of Education, Hamburg. California: Pacific Books.

YOUNG, M. (Ed.) (1965). *Innovation and Research in Education.* London: Routledge and Kegan Paul.